MN00776400

WORSHIP

Essentials For Puja

Meera Sashital

CELESTIAL
BOOKS

ISBN 978-93-81115-49-7
© Meera Sashital, 2011

Design Mishta Roy
Layouts Ajay Shah
Printing Repro India Ltd, Navi Mumbai

Published in India 2011 by
CELESTIAL BOOKS
an imprint of
LEADSTART PUBLISHING PVT LTD
Trade Centre, Level 1
Bandra Kurla Complex
Bandra (E), Mumbai 400 051, INDIA
T + 91 22 40700804
F +91 22 40700800
E info@leadstartcorp.com
W www.leadstartcorp.com

Sales Office
Unit 122, building B/2
Wadala (E), Mumbai 400 037, INDIA
T +91 22 24046887

US Office
Axis Corp
7845 E Oakbrook Circle
Madison, WI 53717, USA

All rights reserved worldwide.
No part of this publication may be reproduced, stored in or introduced into a retrieval system, or transmitted, in any form, or by any means (electorinic, mechanical, photocopying, recording or otherwise), without the prior permission of the Publisher. Any person who commits an unauthorised act in relation to this publication can be liable to criminal prosecution and civil claims for damages.

Disclaimer. The views expressed in this book do not purport to be those of the Publishers.

CONTENTS

Foreword by M.V. Kamath 5
Introduction 7

1. *Aarti* ~ Ritual to Honour & Protect 11
2. *Agarbatti* ~ Incense 14
3. *Akshata* ~ Coloured Rice 19
4. *Ayna* ~ Mirror 22
5. *Chandan* ~ Sandalwood 26
6. *Chavari* ~ Fan 29
7. *Deepak or Jyoti* ~ Sacred Flame 31
8. *Dhol* ~ Drums 35
9. *Ghanta* ~ Bell 39
10. *Haldi* ~ Turmeric 43
11. *Jal* ~ Water 46
12. *Japamala* ~ Rosary 51
13. *Kajal* ~ Collyrium 56
14. *Kalash or Ghata* ~ Pot 58
15. *Kamal* ~ Lotus 62
16. *Karpur* ~ Camphor 67
17. *Kumkum or Sindur* ~ Vermillion 69

18. *Mangal Sutra* ~ Auspicious Cord of Matrimony   72
19. *Manjira or Kafi* ~ Cymbals   75
20. *Om or Aum* ~ Sacred Sound   78
21. *Paan* ~ Betel Leaf   83
22. *Rudraksh* ~ Sacred Seed of Shiva   87
23. *Salagrama* ~ Stone of Vishnu   91
24. *Shankh* ~ Conch   95
25. *Shriphal* ~ Coconut   99
26. *Supari* ~ Betel Nut   102
27. *Swastika* ~ Sacred Symbol   105
28. *Tael or Ghee* ~ Anointing Oil   109
29. *Tulsi* ~ Holy Basil   114
30. *Vibhuti* ~ Sacred Ash   117

Acknowledgements   120
About the Author   121

FOREWORD

The trouble with most post-independence educated people, is that they have been convinced that to be 'secular is the in-thing. Never mind what is sought to be conveyed by the word 'secular', the average secularist presumes that to be a Hindu means being 'communalist'. Hinduism, in certain circumstances, has received a bad name. Many Hindus would be chary of visiting a temple, let alone offering a *puja* at home. With increasing industrialization and the break-up of the joint family, even praying to the family deity or even *ishata devata*, has become passé. Many of the young have no time for such 'spiritual' exercises. It is time to go to the office. It is time to visit the Club. The young Hindu swears by secularism and in effect, rejects many traditional mores.

The contemporary young Hindu needs to be re-aquainted with his past and his *sanatana dharma*, with all that it implies. Part of that task has been boldly undertaken by Meera Sashital. Except on certain important occasions, today's young Hindu does not visit a temple. Of course it is not mandatory. Most homes do have their own *puja* space. Where possible, a room is set apart for this purpose. Prayers on ordinary days may be perfunctory, but at least they are offered. But there are certain days when the entire family – especially a joint family – gathers to offer *puja* and it is then that the requirements of the ritual calls for special attention. What should they be? Coconut or *spriphal*, is a must. To that one can add *paan, supari, haldi, akshata, karpur, tulsi, kumkum* and even a mirror for special occasions. A small bell is essential and if we can add cymbals, it would be even more appropriate. There are other necessities to the occasion such as *saligrama, deepak* to do *aarti*, incense, *chandan* and *vibhuti*, the sacred ash.

Since the puja is generally performed by a professional priest, he would advise on what is needed. And his recommendations have to be met in full. But of what relevance are all these petty things which one ignores in the normal course of things ? This is where Meera Sashital comes into the picture. Every object – *upachara* – has a meaning and relevance, even the humble mirror. For instance, the use of sandalwood paste or turmeric must be seen in their purifiactory function.

God accepts all offerings made by man. Remember what Lord Krishna says in the *Gita*:

patram pushpam phalam toyam yo me bhaktya prayachchhati, tad-aham bhakty-upahritam asnami prayatatmanahi
[If anyone offers me with devotion a leaf, a flower, a fruit, and water, I receive that, offered in devotion by the persons whose soul is disciplined.]

M.V. KAMATH
Mumbai, 2010

INTRODUCTION

From the beginning of time, Man has been filled with awe witnessing the furies of nature – lightning, fire, flood. He felt that somehow these manifestations of nature could be appeased by making offerings to them. Gradually, as civilization advanced and his own intellect grew, Man personified these elements by attributing his own human qualities to them. Fire became Agni; water was Varun; the thunderbolt was Indra and so on. Thus, based on the forces of nature and Man's own qualities, various Gods or deities came into existence.

Man then created images of the Gods or symbols of divinity. He treated them like living personalities and attributing his own likes and dislikes to God. He offered food, flowers, incense and other offerings to these images, as before living beings, after consecrating the images. This kind of offering to divine images after consecration, became the Hindu rituals of Puja or Worship.

The images were given *abhishek* or the ritual bath, then dressed and decorated with ornaments. Man's gratitude and respect for the gods were expressed by offering flowers, fruits, etc. The *diya* or lamp was lit, representing knowledge or the seeking of enlightenment. Incense was burnt to spread fragrance and *aarti* was performed before the images to ward off the evil eye. Perhaps, in ancient times when there was no electricity, this also served as a light to see the divine faces of the images, in the small and dark *garbagriha* or sanctum sanctorum.

Today, Hindu deities are worshipped with *upachara* or articles which are the manifestations of nature or *prakriti*. According to some spiritual leaders, light and food signify trust, adoration, love, knowledge and identity. Hence, we offer to God these articles with complete devotion and reverence as our worship. During the *puja* in a temple, besides the *aarti*, cloth, flowers, conch, chamar, etc., are also symbolically offered.

Every object termed as *upachara*, is offered for a particular purpose. For example, water is essential during *puja* or worship in order to purify the place. *Haldi* or turmeric, Sandalwood paste, anointing, etc. – all have their own significance for purification.

The characteristic offerings in *puja* – flowers, fruits, water, leaves, etc. were unknown to the *homa* or *havan* rite. According to scholars, *puja* is the pre-Aryan or the Dravidian form of worship, while the *homa* is Aryan. Throughout the early period of Vedic literature, there is no mention of the *puja* ritual with flowers etc., offered to an image or symbol of divinity.

The word *puja*, is derived from the root *puj*, and is said to be of Dravidian origin. Mark Collins suggests that the Sanskrit word *puja* (from which the root *puj* was deduced later), was nothing but the Dravidian *pu* or 'flower' plus the root *'get'* meaning 'to do' (palatalized to *je*) – found in Tamil as *chey*, in Kannada as *ge* and in Telegu as *che*. The *puja* ceremony was thus a flower ritual, a flower service, a *pushpa-karma*, just as *homa* was desribed as *pasu-karma* the religious service in which an animal was slaughtered in sacrifice.

According to Jarl Charpentier, *puja* was derived from the Dravidian root *pusu*, meaning 'to smear' – as the smearing of sandalwood paste forms an important item in the *puja* ritual. But the use of blood from a sacrificed animal to anoint anointing stones, was later replaced by red paint or vermillion.

Different religious may have separate ways of making offerings but there is one stream of thought running through them all. The predominant idea behind offerings and prayers as worship or performing *puja*, is the surrender of oneself to that All Powerful, Absolute or Almighty God, in order to seek His blessings, protection and forgiveness. Instead of ceremonial worship, meditational worship is also performed by enlightened spiritual leaders – this is known as *Manas Puja*.

Without going too much into detail, I have tried to explain the essentials or main items used in traditional worship. I hope my readers will find it informative and beneficial in their own worship and surrender to God.

AARTI ~
RITUAL TO HONOUR & PROTECT

The word *aarti* is an indigenous or Dravidian word. In Sanskrit it is called *artrik, artikya, arartikya* or *mahaniranjana*. A flat metal or silver platter with niranjans or tiny containers with lighted wicks, when moved in a clockwise direction before the idol of worship or any person, is known as the act of *aarti*.

While performing *aarti* before images of gods during worship, devotional songs specifically called *aarti*, are sung to the rhythm of cymbals, the ringing of bells and the beating of drums, etc. *Aartis* pertaining to different gods and goddesses are sung to extoll them and pray for their blessings and benevolence. *Aartis* about Lord Ganesha, Lord Shiva, Lord Vithoba, Goddess Durga, Lakshmi Saint Dyaneshwar and others, are some of the more popular ones in Maharashtra.

Aarti performed before temple idols is different from that performed in our daily lives during auspicious occasions or functions. It is a ritual to perform the *aarti* before the idols only after the worship and offerings to them are over. The procedure is to do the *aarti* four times at the feet of the idol, twice at the navel, once in front of the face and seven times before the entire image. There is only a single wick in each *niranjan* and usually there are five *niranjans* on the platter. It is believed that the purpose of the *aarti* is to atone for our misdeeds and seek redemption.

The custom of performing *aarti* has been prevalent since quite early times. Kings, commanders of armies and *pundits* or scholars, were honoured with *aartis*. Originally, *aarti* was believed to ward off the evil eye of spirits, garden imps and evil persons. The same reason extended to *aartis* performed before the gods.

During marriage ceremonies, it is customary to perform *aarti* before the bride and the groom to bring them prosperity and happiness. In Maharashtra, the *aarti* done to a bridal couple is called *kurvadi* and there are specific songs associated with it. Again, during Diwali, at the new moon, wives perform *aarti* to their husbands and on the *Bhavbij* day, sisters do the same for their brothers.

This is all to bring good luck, longevity and happiness to the persons to whom *aarti* is done. Usually, in temples, the *Pujari* or priest performs the *aarti* and at home, the head of the household performs *aarti* to his idols of worship. In social ceremonies, the aarti is generally done by *suhasini* women (whose husbands are alive).

Among the Lingayats, when a man dies, so long as the corpse is in the house, it is the customary for his widow to perform *aarti* in order to prevent her husband's soul from entering the world of spirits.

Again, when a branch of the *Ashwata* (Banyan) tree is cut to kindle the sacred fire before commencing any religious ceremony, *aarti* is performed before the tree, seeking its forgiveness for hurting it. It is also customary to perform *aarti* before digging a well, and to the *Bilva* tree on *Shivaratri*, and at the naming ceremony of a newborn.

It is believed that there is the tremendous cosmic power and divine primal energy infused in the *aarti*. Moreover, it is said to contain the radiance of many Suns and symbolizes Light and Knowledge dispelling Darkness and Ignorance. This is why the *aarti* platter used before deities, is passed amongst the devotees so that they can feel the glow of the flame with their palms and transmit its blessings onto themselves by placing that warmth on their heads. If by some mischance, the *niranjans* fall or the lighted wicks get extinguished while the *aarti* is being done, it is considered inauspicious and religious ceremonies of *shanti* or peace are performed for propitiation and redemption and to avert any untoward incidents in the future.

AGARBATTI ~ INCENSE

Incense has always played an important role in our religion and daily life. The custom of burning fragrant incense has also been widespread and common all over the world. There have been many kinds of incenses. Various substances have been used to produce agreeable colours when burned, such as different kinds of wood or bark, branches or roots of trees, herbs and odoriferous plants, seeds, flowers, fruits, aromatic earths etc. But, Frankincense and other gum resins are more strictly known as incense. The substances referred to in the *Bible* and which are known to have been used by the Hebrews and other people as incense are:

i. **Wood**
   Eagle wood
   Cassia bark
   Cinnamon

ii. **Roots**
   Oostus

iii. **Gum resins**
   Balm (mastic)
   Myrrh (Ladanum)
   Frankincense

iv. **Animal product**
   Anycha (*operculum* of a marine mollusc)

Sacred incense, used in later Hebrew rituals, was a compound of Stacte, Galbanum and pure Frankincense, seasoned with salt and reduced to a fine powder. In later times, the Herodian period, Josephus records that 13 ingredients (sweet-smelling spices), were used. Plutarch gave a list of 16 ingredients used by the Egyptians in preparing *kuphi*. In all these cases, the compounding was of ritual importance and a matter of mystery. Sacred books were read aloud while the *kuphi* was being mixed.

Frankincense is the gum resin of trees of the *genus boswellia*. Pliny referred to it as a product of Arabia and said that the Sabaei tribe alone cultivated the tree which produced it and only by 3,000 families by virtue of hereditary succession. The trees are said to be sacred and while pruning them or gatherings their resin, men are expected to avoid pollution through sexual intercourse or contact with a corpse. Heredotus also wrote of winged serpents which guarded the trees and these were driven off by burning Styrax. It was one of the ingredients of Jewish incense, and is still used in Christian rituals. Classical authors usually refer to Syria and Phoenicia as the original source of Frankincense.

Incense was mainly used because of its aroma. Since ancient times, perfumes have been offered to guests and honoured people and also spread in their paths to keep the air smelling sweet and fresh. Therefore, what was pleasing to Man was presumed to be pleasing to the gods and spirits, just as food that we liked was offered to them. Incense smoke was considered akin to the smoke of the sacrifice that was said to please the gods.

The bodies of the dead are also decked with flowers, aromatic oils and perfumes to keep at bay disagreeable odours. These being obnoxious to man, were thought to be also obnoxious to supernatural beings. Hence, it was surmised that beneficent gods not only liked but actually possessed pleasant aromas themselves.

Incense came to be used in the other ways too because evil odours were known to be obnoxious to the gods as also scared off demons. The pleasant aromas of incense were commonly credited with magical properties. The Andaman islanders believed that the smell of bees' wax was offensive to a demon of epidemics, and is thus kept away by planting stakes in the ground painted with bees' wax. Incense, because it is dreaded by evil spirits, is one of the ingredients of the amulet-box in Tibet. Fumigation is a method of purifying persons and places, and of scaring off all kinds of evil influences. Also, incense is often used in mourning ceremonies in China.

There were other practical, symbolic, or mystical uses served by incense. It was burned to neutralize the strong odours of bloody or burnt sacrifices, especially in hot regions. It was also used for sanitary reasons, in places where the dead were buried. Likewise, it was a symbol or vehicle of prayer. In Egypt it was thought that incense smoke as it rose, bore words of power or prayer to the gods who were pleased by the aroma. The souls of the dead ascended to heaven through the smoke of the incense burned on his behalf. Christians regarded incense smoke as symbolic of prayer, though it also typifies contrition and the preaching of the faith, etc.

The Greek philosopher Plutarch explained the beneficial effects of the Egyptian *kuphi* by saying that its 16 ingredients were aromatic by nature, which lulled people to sleep, loosened the tension of daily anxieties and brightened their dreams. Likewise, resin was supposed to purify the air in the mornings because of its strong and penetrating quality and myrrh at midday dissolved and dispersed the turbid qualities in the atmosphere due to its heat.

India has been famous from ancient times for its perfumes. Incense from Arabia was imported but many native kinds of sweet-smelling materials like Benzoin, and other gum resins, seeds, roots, dried flowers, and fragrant woods have long been in use. These are burned ritually or used for ordinary, domestic purposes. In ancient times sandal-wood was burned as incense. In daily rites, the sacred fire was fed with consecrated wood, usually from the *Palasa* tree. In Hindusim, the use of incense is widespread in all its sects. Camphoras is mostly used to perform *aarti*. *Dhup* is another sweet smelling incense which is burnt before images of gods or in homes to purify the air and spread to fragrance.

Incense was unknown in early Buddhism which preached against external rituals but later, it gradually came into use. In Sri Lanka, perfume and flowers are offered before the image of the Buddha, and in the *Pitri* ceremonial, incense is burned around the platform on which the relics of the Buddha are exposed. But Tibet is the region where incense is most prevalent and travellers have referred to censers like those used by the Roman Catholic Church. Incense is used in the initiation of monks and offered to the good spirits and Lamas in the daily rituals of the monasteries. It is prominent in festivals at which clouds of incense fill the air.

In Japan, incense is commonly used and has influenced the native Shinto religion. In earlier Shintoism, incense was unknown but it is now burned in censers , for example, at the new moon. In China, incense is much used both in public and in private. It is offered before ancestral tablets and household deities and is used in consulting the gods. In Chinese funeral ceremonies, the burning of incense plays an important part, both as an offering and as a fumigatory. The other purpose is to gratify the soul of the deceased.

In Muslims sects, proper incense is not used but it is commonly offered at the shrines of saints and is permitted by tradition to perfume corpses. However, Muslims in India, possibly influenced by Hinduism, use it in their rites such as circumcision, marriage, funerals, etc. and is credited with warding off evil spirits. In Muslim homes it is burnt on braziers whereas in marriage processions it is burnt in a *Mibkharah*, and is commonly used to counteract the evil eye. In the science of *da'wah*, a method of incantation, various perfumes are burnt according to a table showing the letters of the alphabet. The letters of the person's name, for whom the incantation is done, creates the required perfume. The materials used are Frankincense, Benozoin, Styrax, coriander-seeds and also also wood.

Jews thought golden bowls full of incense represented their prayers. Although incense was used in Jewish ceremonials and were two of the offerings of the Magi at the nativity of Christ and its use is referred to in the Apocalypse, there is no evidence that it was part of early church rituals. In fact, there is strong evidence to the contrary and it was almost unknown during the first four centuries. Being a later Jewish usage may also have caused Christians to avoid its use.

In the West, the Ordines of the 8th century describe the swing of the censer during the procession of the Pontiff and his acolytes from the sacristy to the altar in the church at Rome. The use of incense was gradual and its use was not prevalent in the West till the 14th century. In the Roman Catholic Church, incense was burnt at solemn Mass, at blessings, processions, consecration of Churches, burial rites, choral offices etc. In the Church of England, there was no ritual use in Divine services during the period after the Reformation. It was used, however, for sanitary purposes, as a fumigatory, for its agreeable aroma, in churches, at feasts, at coronations etc. Its ritual use was only resumed towards the middle of the 19th century.

AKSHATA ~ COLOURED RICE

Husked rice which is coloured with a mixture of saffron and vermillion is called *akshata*. There are two kinds of *akshata* - one specially consecrated by *mantras* used in religious ceremonies and *pujas* while the other is used as an offering of politeness.

Akshata is also used as a substitution ingredient for rituals and when offerings are absent. In all forms of *puja*, the deities are honoured with *akshata*. By sprinkling *akshata* on the Betal leaf and nut placed before the deities, worship is performed. Though seemingly insignificant in *pujas*, it has its own independent status and honour as an offering to the gods. The *mantra* says:

Akshatastandula: shubhraa: kumkumen virajeeta;
Mayaa nivedita bhavatya grihan parameshwara.
Meaning: The white rice coloured with kumkum means *akshata* which I am devoutly offering to You Oh Parameshwara, please accept it.

During the thread ceremony for boys or in marriage ceremonies, there is the custom of showering *akshata*. At every step of the marriage ceremonial, *akshata* plays a significant part, especially where the consecrated *akshata* is distributed to the guests to shower them on the bridal couple after the exchange of garlands and preceded by chanting of *Mangalashtaka*.

Showering of *akshata* on the bridal couple is an age old custom. The rice is belived to be a symbol of fertility. Hence to bless them with progeny, *akshata* are showered on them. In fact, there are special rituals in the marriage ceremony called *Akshataropan* and *Saash*, where only *suhasini* ladies shower *akshata* on the couple after performing *aarti*.

On the occasion of *Bhav-bij* or *Bhaiya-duj*, sisters place a *tilak* on their brothers' foreheads, along with grains of rice. Then, while performing the *aarti* before their brothers, they shower them with *akshata* mixed with kumkum, in blessing. Allegorically, the showering of *akshata* is the outward expression of wishing someone prosperity and longevity. On all auspicious occasions, *akshata* plays a prominent part. Even on wedding cards we find grains of *akshata* stuck on, to mark the auspiciousness of the event.

From ancient times, people have personified corn as the mother goddess. All agricultural races have applied this idea to their indigenous cereals – if Europe has its Wheat-Mother and Barely-Mother, America has its Maize-Mother and the East their Rice-Mother. The importance of the ritual of the corn, which is observed in connection with indigenous cereals like rice, is founded on the simple concept of rice being animated by a soul like humans. People imagined that in the fibres of the plant, as in the body of man, there is a certain vital element which is separable, called the soul. And, on this theory or myth of the plant-soul, is built the whole worship of cereals.

Many races of the East Indies such as the Kayans of Central Borneo, the Karens of Burma, the Minangkabauers of Sumatra, believe in this rice myth and we too, treat rice with deference. Thus rice is given a spiritual status and used in all our religious ceremonies. Besides this, in the grain fields, rice is thought to have the power to ward off evil, so in order to remove any evil spell cast by the spirits of the fields, the sacred *akshata* is showered.

The *Mangalakshata* can be rice or any other grain. In ancient Greece, wheat flour or sweets were showered. In Persia, rice held an important role during marriage ceremonies and even today, the Parsis follow the custom of showering akshata during marriage or Navjot ceremonies.

Spiritual gurus bless their devotees by giving them *Mantrakshata* as the symbol of prosperity, strength and longevity.

AYNA ~ MIRROR

Mirrors are looked upon with respect and have an honourable place in our rituals and cultural life. The breaking of a mirror is considered most inauspicious.

The word *ayna* has been found to exist in Sanskrit phraseology from ancient times. It is certain that people of those times were familiar with the technique of making mirrors. By polishing any metal, men must have seen their reflections. It is difficult, however, to pinpoint exactly when mirrors began to be used. In an early excavation, among the mirrors found, one was oval shaped and made from an alloy of brass and others metals.

Mirrors, being able to reflect images, naturally created wonder in people's minds and led to superstitious beliefs and practices. It also led to the belief that a person's reflection was his soul. Perhaps, this was one of the reasons why a mirror breaking is considered inauspicious.

Due to superstitions and apprehensions, mirrors were regarded with awe and reverence, hence making an entry into rituals and culture. In Hindu marriages, when receiving the groom's party, the tradition is to carry a mirror on a platter along with *haldi, kumkum*, rose essence, a comb and other accessories, as a toilet kit. There is also the ritual of placing in the left hand of the bride, a mirror, to enable her to dress her hair. In fact, in all auspicious religious ceremonies, a mirror is invariably found to be present amidst other items.

The Andaman islanders regard their reflections in any mirror as their souls. Hindu philosophy has mirror analogies such as, 'The person....that is seen in the eye, that is the Self... This is the Brahman,' from the *Chandogya Upanishad*. Whereas the *Kausitaki Upanishad* states, 'The person that is in the mirror, on him I meditate. ' Fijians and Indonesians have the same belief. To the Melanesians *atai* or soul, meant one's reflection.

There are many weird beliefs about looking at one's reflection in a pool or water. Even Manu, the ancient Indian philosopher, said (in rules for a *snataka*), 'Let him not look at his own image in water.' The old Greeks had the same maxim and we have the story of Narcissus on these lines. Thus, in the simple minds of unsophisticated people, a person's reflection was his spiritual soul and the reflecting surface had somehow abstracted and retained that soul.

With these notions is connected the custom of covering mirrors or turning them to the wall after a death. It was feared that the soul, projected out of the person by his reflection in the mirror, could be carried away. This practice is widespread across Europe and occurs in Islam too. Similarly, sick persons were advised to avoid looking into a mirror, and even in modern Greece, brides are advised to refrain from using a mirror. And it was thought that since the mirror holds the soul, it was extremely unlucky to break a looking glass.

The invention of mirror seems to have taken place with the advent of metallurgy. It was just an adaptation of the polished and reflecting surface of metals. Egyptian mirrors apparently set the mode for all subsequent developments.

Mirrors of ancient times were almost invariably hand-mirrors for ladies toilette purposes. Egyptian mirrors were made of bronze or similar alloys. Mirrors were used in classical Greece and the idea was borrowed by Rome. Both the Greek and the Romans preferred the circular form with handle, as in the Egyptian original. They were usually made of bronze, with 20 to 30 percent of tin. Some were silver plated. The Romans developed the box-mirror, consisting of two round disks joined by a hinge. They also, made large mirrors similar to the modern cheval-glasses and fixed them on walls. By the Christian era, metal mirrors were known in northern India.

During mediaval times, a mirror case continued to be popular among the rich but were small and carried on their person. The largest mirror was as large as a plate and the circular shape was retained. The reflecting surface was usually of polished steel or other metal and steel mirrors were still in the use in the 16th century. Attempts were made with a combination of metal and glass but proved futile. The amalgam of mercury and tin which gives the modern looking-glass its efficiency, came in after the 16th century. Though final improvements were effected in the middle of the 19th century through the invention of plate-glass, it was first in Venice that mirror making acquired its commercial importance.

Many experiments have been conducted with concave and convex effects and were known from early times in both the East and the West. Then there appeared the 'magic mirror' of China and Japan, reflecting on a screen an image of its back. Spherical glass mirrors known as *Ochsenaugen* were present in mediaeval Europe. Mirror-writing also came into prevalence.

Divination by means of a reflecting surface is an ancient, worldwide practice. Its principle was that figures representing present or future souls could be seen. Divination by mirrors is a method of 'seeing' – the most frequent instrument being the crystal ball. In folk tales we read of magic mirrors possessing the power of speech. In *shintoism,* mirrors are actually worshipped. The mirrors have come to represent the divine beings themselves.

The optical properties of the mirror were so important that it came to be used as a metaphor in literature. Buddhist *suttas* speak of 'a way of truth, called the Mirror of Truth'. 'The mirror of the mind' occurs both in Chaucer and in Shakespeare. In Sanskrit mirrors are mentioned often. *Apsaras* and courtesans are shown in sculpture and painting as holding mirrors. Kalidas in his *Kumarsambhav,* has depicted Shiva as presenting a mirror to Parvati. In Tulsidas' *Hanuman Chalisa,* the very first verses narrate the glory of Shri Ramchandra by first cleaning the 'mirror of my heart' with the dust of the *Guru*'s lotus feet.

CHANDAN ~ SANDALWOOD

Sandalwood or *Chandan*, is a fragrant evergreen tree belonging to the *genus Santalum*. It is also known as *Gandhasar* and *Malayaj*. In India, Coorg, Andhra Pradesh, Karnataka, the Nilgiris, south Maharashtra and especially Mysore, are full of sandalwood trees. The species are native to India, Malaysia, Australia and Polynesia. Their fragrant wood contains an oil that is extracted for use in perfumery. The name sandalwood refers primarily to the white variety of Sandalwood, *Santalum album*, a tree native to India. This evergreen tree grows in red or a hard soil.

Sandalwood is an item which is invariably utilized in our rituals and *pujas*. Sandalwood paste is used to anoint the idols of the gods. The fragrant sandal-paste is offered with *haldi* and *kumkum* to ladies on auspicious occasions. During marriage ceremonies, sandalwood is used extensively. The bridal couple are anointed with sandal-paste and turmeric after their customary oil bath. Sandalwood water or rose-water is offered to the guests and this custom of *malaya-chandana* is the ancient *arghya*.

In death, the body is washed and anointed with sandal-paste besides oil and turmeric.

In temples, after the idols are bathed, they are anointed with sandal paste. The priest also applies sandal paste or *chandan* to the idol's forehead. Priests and sages have the sandalwood paste *tilak* on their foreheads and also on their bodies. The Vaishnavites in particular use sandalwood paste only for the traditional sacred markings on their faces and limbs. During coronations of *Rajahs* in India, a mixture of sandal paste and *attar* of roses, was the unguent applied with the middle finger of the right hand on the forehead of the kings. Sacred stones like the Shiva *linga* also have sandal-paste applied to them.

Besides religious purposes, sandalwood has been used for cosmetics and soaps and in the medicinal field too. The hard wood of the white sandalwood tree has a lasting fragrance which is used for cabinet work, carving and perfumery. The tree has leaves that are two inches (five centimeters) long, yellow flowers that turn red, and a black fruit. Other unrelated trees, some with a similar odour, are also called sandalwood. *Myoporum sandwicence*, has a fragrant wood and is native to Hawali. It grows to 60 feet (18 metres) and has leaves six inches (15 centimeters) long with white or pink flowers and white fruit.

Sandalwood has been classified into three colours, viz, white, red and yellow. Red sandalwood is called *Raktachandan* or *Pierocarpus santalinus*, is an odorless wood which produces a red dye. *Raktachandan* is noted more for its medicinal values.

As mentioned earlier, *attar* or perfumes are made from sandalwood tree oil. Mysore is well known for its sandalwood articles and oil. Due of its cooling effect, sandalwood paste is applied to the forehead and its oil is applied on the head. Banbhatta has mentioned white *chandan* in his poems while describing how women suffering the pangs of separation from their lovers, applied *chandan* or sandalwood paste to their bodies to reduce their agonies. Reptiles too, curl round sandalwood trees for coolness.

A famous couplet in Hindi literature describes how Saint Tulsidas, a devotee of Lord Rama, sat at Chitrakut *ghat*, making sandalwood paste while praying for *darshan* or vision, of Lord Rama. But, Saint Tulsidas was so engrossed in his devotion and his work that when Lord Rama actually came, Tulsidas unconsciously applied *tilak* of *chandan* on Lord Rama's forehead without recognizing him – realizing it too late when Lord Rama vanished.

CHAVARI ~ FAN

Long before the age of electricity, Man depended on natural breezes to cool him the scorching sun or humid heat. But in the absence of breezes, people created artificial breeze by waving a large leaf to keep cool.

The early Assyrians and Egyptians used hand fans made of palm leaves. In India too, hand fans have been used since ancient times. Fans were made from the long leaves of palm trees, split and interwoven into small mats, keeping the required portion of the branch to form the handle. In south India specially, these fans are very popular.

The *chavari* evolved as kings, queens and dignitaries required more sophisticated fans. The *chavari* is made from the tail hair of an animal called *Chaamar*. Hence it is also called *chaamari*. It is also made from the tail hair of the Yak. The *chavari* is mounted on a handle made from either gold, silver or ivory. *Chavaris* were more befitting for kingly use because of their exquisite beauty and elegance.

Not only in India, but also all over Asia, it is the custom to hold umbrellas over kings and to use *chavaris* to fan them.

From ancient times the umbrella and the *chavari* have been acknowledged as symbols of great honour and prestige. The *chavari* became an item symbolizing the qualities of divinity, prosperity and royalty, meant for kings and spiritual men. Hence they were reserved for people of importance and distinction. Lord Buddha, however, prohibited his monks or *bhikus* from using the *chavari* as he thought it was, besides being a luxury, a privilege of kings and nobles.

It has always been the nature of human beings to attribute our wants and feelings to the gods. Hence, during worship, one of the rituals is waving of the *chavari* over the deities.

In temples and *gurudwaras,* before the *aarti,* the *chavari* is waved. Again, when the deities are taken out in a procession, they are always fanned with *chavaris.* Fans were also used to brush flies from sacred vessels in the Christian Church from about 300 to 1300 AD.

Before the advent of electricity, it was customary for wives to wait on their husbands by fanning them while they ate or rested. Whether the family was rich or humble, it was obligatory for a devoted wife to sit near her husband and see to his comforts especially while dining and resting using a hand fan. However, in wealthy homes there were huge leaves or *pankhas* tied to ropes which were pulled by *pankhawallas,* to create a cool breeze while the wealthy homeowners rested.

Today, hand fans are made from many other materials besides palm leaves. Fans made from bamboo are found in various shapes, sizes and colours in different parts of India. Folding hand fans are also made from sandalwood and plastic too.

Historians believe that the folding fan was invented in Japan in about 700 AD. It is probable that the fan was made after noticing the way in which a bat folds its wings. The Japanese often use them in ceremonial dances. The Chinese also began using folding fans and in the 1500s, the Portuguese took it to Europe where it immediately became the fashion.

DEEPAK or JYOTI ~ SACRED FLAME

There is saying about the *deepak* or flame lit before deities, *Deepayate deepayati va svam paremcheti*, meaning: '*Deepak* which gives light and brightness to itself; gives illumination to others'.

Light is another form of fire or *agni*. It was one of the earliest discoveries of Man and has always been looked upon as sacred. Fire was later used in sacrifices to propitiate the gods and thus it entered the religious realm. Light destroyed darkness and had the integral power of the sun's brilliance. Even the shining moon and the twinkling stars threw light in darkness and brightened the path of the wanderer. Men worshipped the sun, moon, stars and lightening – perceiving them as super-natural elements and revering them with awe.

Man worshipped *jyoti* or a flame because it consumed impurities and yet remained pure. To mankind light signified brightness, knowledge, wisdom and purity. Darkness meant ignorance, evil, fear and impurity. Thus, quoting from the *Upanishads*, man prayed, *Tamaso ma Jyotigamaya* (Lead me O kindly light! Lead me from darkness to light). The lighted flame was always within reach to protect people, unlike the sun and moon. Fire or flame was mankind's eternal companion. Thus light was extremely sacred to all.

The *Skanda Purana* says, 'Fire burns up everything whereas a lamp or *Diya* destroys darkness and spreads light'. Priests lit the lamp or *diya* (*deepak*) before the deities to brighten the *sanctum sanctorium* and seek blessings. The *deepak* being a symbol of brightness and knowledge is one of the main items in rituals during worship. No *puja* is ever performed without lightning a *diya*. In every home, morning and evening, the *diya* is lit before the family deity. In the evenings when the lamp is lit children are taught to recite the important *slokas* or verses, addressed to the lamp which conclude with *Deepam Jyothi Namostuthe* which are salutations to the lamp.

During *pujas* or auspicious functions, the diya is regarded as witness and is part of the *aarti*. The flame is considered to be the source of infinite energy so devotees extend their palms over the flame of the *aarti* to feel its heat and be blessed by its aura. Even scientists have experimented with the use of a flame to cure certain ailments as it serves as killer of germs.

In temples of Vishnu and Pandurang, early morning *aarti* is performed daily before the deity and is called the *Kakad Aarti*. Similarly at night, before putting the god to sleep, *aarti* called *shejaarti* is performed. In the temples of Shiva, the *diya* is kept burning continuously for eight hours and is called *nandadeep*.

The *diya*, being regarded as a symbol of auspiciousness, it is part of the *aarti* performed before newly-wed couples to bless them with long happy married life. Again, during *Diwali*, on *Bhaubeej* day, the sister performs *aarti* before her brother to wish him long life. When a person leaves home on some mission, the *diya* is once more part of his send-off. The custom of *aarti* is considered a good omen, drives away evil and brings good luck, protection and long life.

In one of Kalidasa's works, there is mention of *aarti* being done even to the horses. During Diwali, on the *Polya* ceremony day, bulls, and on the new moon day the cows and their calves, have *aarti* performed to them to ensure their safety.

When pilgrims visit holy places, they place lighted wicks in leaf cups and float them in sacred rivers as offerings to the river.

There are some rules and restrictions which are supposed to be strictly observed. For example, a lamp lit before a deity should not be stolen; a lighted *diya* should not be blown off with one's breath and a lighted *diya* should not be dropped as this is considered an ill omen.

Originally, a diya was an oval shaped, pointed, small, earthen container. It was filled with *ghee* or clarified butter and a twisted cotton taper immersed in it and the end lit. With the development of art, many designs of *diyas* came into use. One such was the *deevriksha*, designed as a tree with branches and having small depressions to put in the oil and wicks. Then there are those beautifully designed with chains for hanging. The tall *diyas* with petals for lighted wicks and adorned with a peacock, are often used for opening ceremonies. Then there is the *Panchayat* which is held by five *suhasinis*, women whose husbands are alive. *Diyas* in the shape of snakes with a plate on the hood for lighted wicks, are also popular. There are numerous designs of *diya*.

As we have seen, the deepak as an element giving ligh,t has holds a strong place in our religious observations. Even Lord Shiva advised Parvatii to always light a lamp. To make a *deep daan* or offer a gift of lighted *diyas*, is considered to gain great merit. In the month of *Kartik*, to light *diyas* before Lord Vishnu, is said to be the equal of making a full pilgrimage, as well as offering oblations to the departed souls.

Christians carry candles and light them to pray in churches. Zorastrians consider the flame sacred. The sun, the greatest luminous heavenly body visible to us, and fire are specially regarded and extolled as the representatives of *Ahura Mazda*.

It is aid that once the setting sun asked, 'Who will take up my work?' None came to answer. But an earthen lamp humbly said, 'I will, my Lord, as best as I can.' Just as a lamp in windless places does not flicker, similarly the disciplined mind of a *yogi* can concentrate on God without being distracted.

DHOL ~ DRUMS

The drum is a percussion instrument made from a hollow cylindrical or hemispherical frame of wood or metal, with a head of tightly stretched membrane at one or both ends. By striking this stretched area, a distinctive sound is produced.

The actual genesis of the membrane-drum cannot be traced but is thought to have been independently invented by a many races. Primitive people drummed their fists on hollow tree-trunks to frighten away wild animals or spirits. With special techniques of drumming, entire villages were quickly summoned to face a common danger or to take part in their ritual dances. To these people, drumming and rhythm became part of incantation and magic.

Primitive man discovered rhythm from the movements of his own body. If we listen to any piece of music, we still find there is a regular beat behind it to which we automatically tap or clap. The marching song for instance, inspires due to its regular rhythm.

Early peoples were known to have marked the rhythm by beating their hands on their chests, flanks or bellies.

The Andamanese women beat time for dancers by slopping the hollow between the thighs as they sat squat on their heels. Another method common to several races is to use a bundle of skins tied into a package and then to beat this with a stick. In Australia, Possum skin was often used as the membrane stretched to form the drum head.

The importance of the drum is connected to its being the chief and sometimes only musical instrument. The structural variations of the drum are many, but eight types are clearly marked:

i.   the incision drum
ii.   the stamping drum
iii. the single-headed membrane drum
iv.   the double-headed membrane drum
v.   the friction-drum
vi.   the pot drum
vii. the kettle drum
viii the tambourine

Drums in different forms are seen and heard all over the world. However, there are more varieties of drum in Africa than anywhere else and are sometimes unique or extremely rare.

The drum is of great antiquity. In India findings in the Indus Valley excavations unearthed different kinds of highly developed drums (one of them just like the present *mridangam*). It was known in Vedic India and a hymn in the *Atharvaveda* sings its praises. Early Chinese records also mention the drum. The Assyrians and the Egyptians used the tambourine and the double-headed drum. The latter was supported against the drummer's body and played with both hands.

In *vedic* India the drum was also invoked to drive away danger, demons and enemies. It was used in sacrifices and in battle; warriors worshipped it. Before being played, a *mantra* or charm was spoken into it. The analogy between thunder and the boom of the drum is very clear. In the great Oriental religions, particularly Hinduism and Buddhism, the drum has an important place in the temple-worship. It is not unknown in Islamic worship. Russian peasants, used the drum to imitate thunder and produce rain.

Even today, drums and other allied percussion instruments, play a significant part in our religious functions, social activities and cultural festivities. Our Indian drum the *dhol*, is always played while *aarti* is performed during Saraswati and other *pujas*. The *dhak* is the bigger version of the *dhol* and is used in Durga and Kali *puja* celebrations.

In the north, the *dholak* is played by women folk on the occasions of *sagai* or the engagement ceremony, *mehandi*, marriage and other auspicious functions accompanied by songs. *Khol*, mostly used in Manipuri dances, is an elongated drum in the shape of the *Mridangam* and is horizontally hung on a man's neck and played with both hands while dancing. In south India, there is the *Mridangam* and the *Ghatam* which are used for accompaniment but are also played in temples. The *Pakhawaj* is another variety which is used in the classical Dhrupad and Dhamars styles of music. The jazz drum is the latest percussion instrument used in modern music. And who does not know of Lord Shiva holding the *Damaru*, the hand drum in his dancing pose?

The use of the drum as a social instrument and the skill of drum-playing, have their higher development in Africa. Drum playing requires considerable skill, particularly because of the rebound of the membrane. It is in the utilization of this rebound that the skill of the drummer lies. Drumming is closely connected to our emotions and muscular movements. It is complete enough in itself to cover the whole range of human feeling. Rhythm is almost a neuro-muscular quality and it is the fundamental form of musical sound.

The drum has been put to a multitude of uses besides military, religious and social. In central Africa, the drum besides being used as an instrument of social intoxication, religious ceremonies and exhortations of the sick, plays the part of the church-bell, the clock, the town-crier and the daily newspaper. From early times and even today, the drum has been the instrument which announces both joy and sorrow. It was used to make Royal proclamations, public announcements and mourning of the dead. It gave the alarm for war and also the return of the brave triumphant warriors. It is the drum that unifies the rhythm and tempo of the marching army. Drums were carried on journeys and beaten to encourage walkers as also to scare away wild animals. Villagers would use the drum to exchange signals and transmit news. Its most spectacular use was as a postal, telegraphic and telephonic service.

Be it a religious procession during *pujas*, marriage processions or *baraats* and even during political campaigns, drummers lead the way. The drummer inspires, leads and represents human emotion and movement. The sound of the drum is not merely sound, but a spiritual reverberation.

GHANTA~ BELL

A mong most races, the bell has been a useful percussion instrument, especially in the religious domain. When the clapper strikes the metal inside wall, it produces a sonorous vibration throughout the entire circumference.

The origin of the bell is traced by scholars to Asia, during the bronze or iron age. The new metal iron was considered powerful and its use prophylactic. Man discovered that a more resonant note could be obtained by striking the edge of metal pots rather than an iron bar. Thus, man's visualization and invention led to this convenient upside down cup with a clapper inside and a handle.

The earliest use of bells was prophylactic and people made use of sounds produced by gongs to scare away beasts, give warnings or convey messages. Later, bells were found to be more convenient than gongs. Early Man believed in demons and his superstitious mind told him that ringing bells would drive away evil forces and safeguard him.

Primitive people also devised bells of wood, shell and other materials of little resonance, but in later civilizations, resonant bronze alloys prevailed. The alloy commonly known as bell metal, contains approximately three to four parts copper to one of tin. Most Western bells have a characteristic tulip shape but in China and elsewhere ,bells of rectangular, beehive, ecliptical and other shapes, were common.

In most religions bells play an important part. Every Hindu temple entrance has a hanging bell. It is customary for every person entering to ring the bell. It is a symbolic way of announcing to God that one has come to seek His blessings and protection. In Hinduism, a *ghanta* or hand bell is a must during worship or for rituals. The *ghanta* remains permanently before the family or temple deities. Before commencing the *puja*, the bell is worshipped first and is intermittently rung while chanting certain portions of the *mantras*. The ringing bell symbolizes the driving away of evil influences.

The *sloka* says:
Panchlohamayi ghanta rudrasyalhadkarini, snane dhoope cha deepe cha ghandernadmachreth.
Meaning : The Panchlohi *ghanta* being Rudra's favourite, while performing *abhishek*, lighting incense, the *deep* or *aarti*, ring the sound of the bell.

Indian bells have special importance of their own. They are of various kinds and are considered weapons of different gods. When the handle has a diamond, the *ghanta* is called *Vajraghanta*, which is belived to symbolize the material and spiritual cosmos. Sometimes the handle is shaped like *garuda*, the vehicle of Lord Vishnu, and is called *Garuda ghanta* and is thus loved by Lord Vishnu. There is a belief that the *Garuda ghanta* protects man from serpents, fire and lightning. There are other *ghantas* with the tops of the handle shaped like Hanuman, a serpent, a *chakra* or wheel etc. The resonance of the *ghanta* is supposed to please all the gods and drive away demons.

Thus, according to the *Brahamans* in Hinduism, two things are indispensable to the worshipper or devotee – a lighted lamp or *diya* and a bell to wake the divinity from sleep so that he may accept the offerings made.

In Buddhism, bells and gongs play a large part in religious ceremonies. The noise made during certain rites is quite deafning, the object being to call the attention of the divinity to the prayers and ceremonies of the devotees. The suspension of a number of bells in order to tinkle in the wind, is considered to be prophylactic and to scare away demons. Buddhist theogony is almost identical to the *Brahminical*. In Lhasa, the more saintly Lamas wear a tinkling bell on the crown of their hats. Hand bells are also placed upon the altar, perhaps to attract god's attention.

In Burma, great bells are found at most shrines. Just as in the Hindu religion *ghantas* are considered auspicious, in Buddhism and Jainism, bells are compulsory in the temples. *Stupeghanta* is considered most sacred.

Bells have long been employed in Christian churches and have always been associated with religious services. Here too, bells are hung or suspended and have great sanctity Bells are rung to summon worshippers to prayer; they also provide all manner of community signals like alarms and warnings of approaching danger or are rung in celebration to announce births, victory in wars or grand events.

It is said a huge bell was brought by the Portuguese to India. When the Marathas overpowered the Portuguese, they found many bells, some of which we find hung in Hindu temples. The *Naroshankari* bell at the Rameshwar temple in Nasik and the bell hung at the Bhimashankar temple, are some examples. Bells are treated with such reverence that one must be careful not to drop one. Bells are hung on animals such as cows to ward off evil and protect them from harm. The rattle with bells given to a child, was perhaps originally meant to ward off evil elements. Bells are also used for practical purposes such as on fire engines, railway stations, educational institutions and factories.

The only religion which does not use bells and in fact has an aversion to them, is Islam. Muslims do not use bells because of their association with Christianity and have a prejudice against gongs as they are supposed to disturb the dead. Ironically, during the reign of the Mughal Emperor Jehangir, who was noted for his strong sense of justice, had a Chain of Justice put up outside his palace and this chain carried 60 bells which could be shaken by the poorest of his subjects to bring to his notice a grievance or plea for justice.

Bells have grown from the modest sizes first known in the 11th century to that of the King of Bells at Moscow, said to be 20 feet 7 inches high with a diameter of 22 feet and a circumference of over 63 feet (19.2 meters). Its weight has been estimated at 4,32,000 pounds (196,400 kg). Having fallen from its support in a fire in 1737, when a piece was broken from it, the bell was raised up again in 1836 and placed on a support and used as a tiny chaplet.

Bells were introduced into France in 550AD and to England about a century later. One of the oldest bells in Great Britain is the Bell of Saint Patrick's Will ay Belfast. It is 15 centimeters high and 13 centimeters across. According to legend, this bell once belonged to St. Patrick.

Another famous bell, Big Ben, hangs in Westminster Clock Tower in London. China's most famous bell is in Beijing. It weighs 54 metric tons and was made in 1420. In Burma there is a 72 metric ton bell. The most famous bell in America is the Liberty Bell in Philadelphia. It pealed forth the news of the signing of the Declaration of Independence.

Bells have often been used in musical compositions. Nicholas Dalayrac introduced bells in his opera *Camille*. Bells have been used in Rajasthani folk dances in India, which greatly enriches the beauty of the dance and the musical experience.

HALDI ~ TURMERIC

*H*aldi or turmeric, forms an important item in our religious ceremonies and worship. It comes from the powdered tubers of the *Curcuma longa*, classified under the *Zingiberaceae* root family.

Turmeric is a perennial Asian plant, cultivated for its yellow tuberous root. The turmeric plant has narrow leaves one to one-and-a-half feet. (30-45 cm) long. The pale yellow flowers are borne on spikes four to seven inches (10-18 cm) long. When the tuberous roots are dried and ground, it forms the turmeric powder which is widely used as a spice in cooking.

Turmeric achieves importance because it features largely in Hindu ceremonials. During all *pujas,* turmeric, along with betel nut, is offered to the deities. During religious functions like *Haldi-Kumkum, suhagan* or married ladies apply *Haldi-Kumkum* on their foreheads and are offered a betel leaf, betel nut and a piece of *Haldi*. Before performing *Gauri Puja* or any other *Devi Puja* (worship of the goddess), married women apply turmeric powder while bathing as it is considered auspicious and a purifier.

The practice of smearing the face with the turmeric powder is widely prevalent. It is believed to bring longevity and prosperity. In some communities, after the *sagai,* which is the engagement ceremony, the *Ghari Pujan* is performed at both the bride's as well as the groom's houses, when *suhagan or* married women, grind wheat and pound turmeric to symbolize that rejoicing has begun and food has to be prepared for the guests.

Before the wedding, an oil and turmeric paste mixture is rubbed onto the face, feet, hands and spine, of both the bride and groom. This event is one of the important rituals of the marriage. The bride and the groom are also bathed in turmeric water to sanctify them. Again, to ward off the evil eye, a vessel containing turmeric water is waved in front of the bridal couple at weddings.

In various Indian communities, the important and binding part of the marriage rites is the tying together of the hands of the bride and groom with a cotton thread dyed with turmeric, silk thread or sacred *dhruba* grass.

Family life is very strongly rooted in the island of Java. The people are prolific and rejoice over the birth of every child. Wives are treated with much kindness, sons and daughters with great tenderness. When a Javanese woman is pregnant, they offer her presents of rice dyed yellow with turmeric. During the seventh month of pregnancy, a feast is given to relatives and friends, at which the dish of rice stained yellow with turmeric, the colour considered to bring good luck, is never omitted from the menu.

In the Carolines, the clothing of the menfolk consist of beautiful woven girdles of vegetable fibre while their costume for ceremonial occasions is a petticoat of coconut leaves. These leaves are cut into narrow strips and soaked to make them supple and then dyed with turmeric to look bright yellow.

Turmeric is also used to colour food and cloth and in chemistry, the powder is used to indicate the presence of an acid. The dried tubers yield oil of *curcuma*, used for flavoring and occasionally as a perfume ingredient.

Turmeric powder or *haldi* is used liberally in cooking. The turmeric leaves are of great use as wrappers to make pancakes. The batter of refined flour or *maida* is spread on the leaf. On the batter a mixture of coconut and jaggery is placed as a filling. The leaf is then folded and steamed to make delicious sweet pancakes.

Turmeric has its medicinal properties too. *Haldi* in hot milk brings relief from coughs. It is used also as a disinfectant and in poultices.

Above all, *haldi* is used as a cosmetic by women to improve their complexion. Mixed with slaked lime, its powder which becomes red, called *kumkum*, is applied by married women to their foreheads. A privilege exclusive to them – widows are not allowed to use this.

Given its varied uses, turmeric occupies an important, useful and revered place in our daily lives.

JAL ~ WATER

Water or *jal,* and air, are the two indispensable elements in our lives. Water has been traced to creation or the beginning of life. The book of *Genesis* maintains that water was the first element to appear during the initial three days of creation. The *Upanishads* too, uphold that water was the root of all life. According to the ancient Egyptian religion, the Lord of All rose out of the watery mass much before heaven, earth and any creatures came into existence. Thales, the philosopher, considered water to be the central principle or element of cosmology. The *Vedas* term fire *apam-napat* or 'son of the waters', in the belief that fire is produced from water.

To man, water meant purity and cleanliness. Owing to its immeasurable utility and importance, water became an object of worship. It became a symbol of sanctity in almost every religion. The *Vedas* deified and honoured water as 'mother of the earth'. No Hindu religious ceremony is conducted without the medium of water. The *ghata* or *kalasa* (jug of water), with five mango leaves and a coconut on top, is always installed before the commencement of a *puja*. The *kalasa* symbolizes the gods or goddesses being worshipped – different parts of it representing gods like Vishnu, Brahma and so on. The seven sacred rivers are said to be present in the water of the *ghata*.

The usual preliminary to all Hindu religious rites is the sipping of water called *achman*. Water is placed in the hollow of the palm of the right hand and two or three mouthfuls sipped. This is done for internal ablution and is meant to cleanse the body and soul. It is done at the commencement *of Sandhya Vandan,* when the 24 principal names of the god Vishnu are invoked. Every devout Hindu, before partaking of any food, also performs *achman* also and then sprinkles the water around his plate, speaking a grace or prayer.

The act of *arghya* also consists in offering water in a vessel to a Brahmin or a guest. The *tarpana* ceremony comprises offering water as refreshment to the gods, sages and departed souls. Here, water is taken in the cup of the right hand and poured out over the straightened fingers in three different ways. This act signifies the *Deva* (gods), *Rishi* (sages) and *Pitri* (forefathers) *tarpanas.*

During a Hindu marriage, a *ghatika* or a water-clock, is consulted to obtain the accurate *muhurat* (auspicious time) to perform the ceremony. Again, in the *Madhuparka* ceremony, water is used to wash the feet of the bridegroom and the guests. Above all, in a *Kanyadaan* (giving away of the bride), regarded as the most meritorious act in one's life, or any *daan* (offering), is performed with water and a *Tulsi* leaf. During *Kanyadaan,* the hands of the bride are placed over those of the groom and water is poured over their hands by the father of the bride, denoting the gifting of his daughter to the groom.

On auspicious occasions a plate with water and vermillion mixed, is placed before a person to ward off evil. In the *sanskaras* or rites which a Hindu observes from birth to death, water is always used for purification, including after confinement, death etc. Similarly, in the Shinto religion in Japan, the cleaning rite or *misogi,* with water, is intended to remove accidental defilement acquired by contact with unclean things, ranging from simple dirt to the pollution of death and disease, much as Hindus do. In Christian Baptism, water takes precedence in the purification rites.

Among Hindus, it is customary to sprinkle a few drops of Ganges water into the mouth of a dying person. Also, the *ashthi* (ashes), of a dead person is put into the Ganges or other holy rivers. The *shraddha* or funeral rites, of departed souls, are often performed on the banks of holy rivers.

The idols worshipped in homes and in temples, are given daily baths as purification, known as *abhishek*. The *Mahamastakabhishek*, given to the Gomateshwara idol at Shravanabelagol (Mysore), once in twelve years, is an occasion of great celebration.

The seven most sacred rivers according to the *Bhagvata Purana*, are the Ganges, Jamuna, Saraswati , Indus, Sindh, Godavari, Narmada and Kaveri. A dip in these river waters is said to cleanse and expiate all sins. Each river has its own importance and place in mythology with legends associated with it. Many *tirthas* or places of pilgrimage, have sprung up on their banks and in the vicinities of these holy rivers. The confluence of the Ganges with the Jamuna and Saraswati (invisible), called the Triveni Sangam, is one of the most hallowed spots in India.

A common but significant practice among pilgrims is to bring water from the Ganges at Benaras and pour it over the Shiva Linga at Rameshwaram and then have a bath at Dhanushkoti. Similarly, waters from the sources of the Jamunotri and Gangotri, are carried to Kedarnath temple to perform *abhishek*.

There are several wells in India which have a mythological background. Many of these are connected and associated with the wanderings of Ram and Sita during their exile from Ayodhya. The Manikarnika well at Banaras is believed to have sprung up when an earring of Lord Shiva fell into it. It is said that those who drink its waters gain wisdom. In a similar fashion, the well of Zumzum in Mecca, is held in great reverence by the Muslims. A bath with its water is believed to remove all sins. Again, the spring at Lourdes, France, has been credited with miraculous healing powers and is a famous place of pilgrimage. A peasant girl named Bernadette Soubirous, claimed to have experienced visions of the Virgin Mary in a grotto near the spring.

Waters of some lakes have also been held sacred. While describing to Bhishma the greatness of various *tirthas* (pilgrimage spots), Sage Pulastya listed lake Pushkar, popularly known as Pushkar Raja, as the foremost. Lord Brahma is said to dwell here eternally and is worshipped by gods and demons alike. Another lake of fame is the Mansarovar in Tibet. This lake was supposed to have been formed from the mind of Lord Brahma, hence the name. Even a sip of this water is said to redeem a person from sin and grant him *moksha* (liberation). It is stated that a person bathing in the lake of gods in Kalinjar, acquires merit equal to that of making a gift of 1,000 cows.

During times of famine or drought, water is widely used in ceremonies to attract rain. In Australia, a group of people have water for their totem, and their chosen leader, a rain-maker residing in the rain country, holds an assembly to make himself an ally of water power and to befriend the rains. Till recently, in France, images of saints were dipped in water to bring rain, just like the statue of Buddha is drenched with water when there is drought.

Water is the main theme in many of our festivals. For example, *Holi*, signifying the advent of spring, is chiefly marked by the squirting of coloured water on each other. In Mayanmar (Burma), the spring festival is observed in a similar way but unlike Holi, plain water is used. On *Narali Purnima* or Coconut Day, on the full moon day of the month of *Shravan* which marks the end of the monsoons, the main festivity consists in offering coconuts to the sea or rivers, as a mark of gratitude to Lord Varuna, the sea-god.

In Japan, New Year's day is the first event for which water is drawn at daybreak, if possible from a well or a neigbouring stream, and is known as 'young water'. This, it is believed to have the effect of preserving good health throughout the year. Again, on the early morning of seventh day of the New Year, all the decorations within and outside the house are taken down and either burnt or thrown into the sea as a token of purification. It is for the same reason that in Hindu religious festivals, the idols of worship are immersed in the sea or rivers at the end of the celebrations.

Water has been used as an instrument of magic, charm and spells from olden times. In the *Puranas* and Epics, we come across instances when short-tempered sages sprinkled water from their *Kamanadal* on persons they wanted to cast a spell upon or curse or even to fulfill boons. In mythology, Bhagiratha, by his severe austerity, propitiated Brahma and Shiva and brought the Ganges to earth to water the ashes of the 60,000 sons of Sagara and restore them to life, purified by the sacred water from all their sins. The sons of Sagara had been turned to ashes by the wrath of Sage Kapila. In another story, to test the chastity of Anasuya, Brahma, Vishnu and Shiva visit her in the garb of *sanyasis* (holy men) but are only willing to accept her alms if she offers it in the nude. To maintain her *Pativrata Dharma*, Anasuya sprinkles water on them and transforms the Trimurti (Trinity) into babies.

Among the Hindus, the god of water, called Raja Kidar (Indianised from Khwaja Khizr), is supposed to be the patron saint of the water of immortality. Hindus and Muslims alike invoke his help and protection when their boats are adrift.

During floods, offerings are made to rivers and seas to propitiate their spirits and make the waters recede. No wonder then, that the importance of water in our rituals has been glorified in the scriptures and hymns of praise sung in its honour.

JAPMALA ~ ROSARY

A rosary or *japmala*, is a string of beads used as an aid to memory, concentration and for counting, while reciting one's prayers. When repeating the names of god, the rosary helps one to keep count of the number of times the words have been recited. The beads can be made of wood, metal, stone or seeds. The use of the rosary is very popular worldwide but its origin and antiquity is traced to Asia. The rosary is used in a number of religious including Hinduism, Buddhism, Islam and Christianity.

It is thought that the Hindus were the first to evolve the rosary. Called *japa-mala* in Sanskrit, it is sometimes known as *smarani* 'remembrance', because of its aid in counting prayers. A person repeats the name of god while he turns the rosary and counts the beads. This method of counting and praying is used not only by sages but by many people to strngthen concentration.

The rosary differs according to the sect to which the user belongs. The material the beads are from also have specific significance. The number of beads on a rosary varies according to the sect. A Shiva worshipper has 32 beads or double that number in his rosary, whereas a follower of Vishnu has 108 beads in his rosary.

The material used as beads by Shaivites is the well-known *rudrakasha,* considered to be the eye of the god Rudra (Shiva). *Rudrakasha* generally comes from *Eleocarpus ganitrus.* The facets or slits running from end to end of each seed have been given much importance and are called *mukhs* or mouths. A one-mouthed *rudraksha* is considered to be the most scared. According to legend, the seeds are said to be the tears of Rudra (Shiva), which fell either when he was in a rage or in grief and which crystallized.

The worshippers of Vishnu, on the other hand, use rosaries with *Tulsi* seeds (holy Basil – *Ocimum sanctum*), because this plant is sacred to Lord Vishnu. While telling the beads, the rosary is rotated only with the thumb and the middle finger, leaving the forefinger free. Generally, the number of beads in a rosary is 108. In Hindusim, this figure carries great importance, because the number of *Upanishads* is said to be 108. Furthermore, in the *Mahabharata,* the names of Lord Vishnu and Lord Shankar (Shiva), are also given as 108. Actually the rosary need contain only 9 beads but to make the repetition 12 times, 108 beads are put in.

Generally, while telling his beads, the individual conceals his hand with the rosary in a bag or covered with a clot, to evade the eyes of onlookers. Perhaps this is done to preserve its sanctity and avoid evil influences. The bag which is of a particular shape, is called *gaumukhi* or 'cow's mouth'. The *mantra* repeated could be the *Gayatri* from the *Rig Veda* or a *mantra* given by a Guru during initiation.

The rosary plays a prominent part in the ceremony when an adult is initiated by a Guru or a child undergoes the Sacred Thread or *Upanayan* ceremony. The Guru sits with the disciple under a cloth canopy and whispers the holy *mantra* (sacred formula) into the disciple's ear – the disciple repeat this *mantra* daily using his rosary. It is not conditional that only initiated people should use the rosary. Anyone with a religious inclination can do so. To count the prayers, fingers are also used, known as *karamala*. Another Hindu rosary, the *baijantimala* (*baijanti* meaning flag or standard) for Vishnu worshippers, consists of five gems produced from the five natural elements: sapphire from the earth, pearl from water, ruby from fire, topaz from the air, and diamond from ether or space.

Devotees attach great importance to the size of the beads – the larger they are, the more effective the rosary and greater the merit attained by the user. When expensive rosaries with the requisite number of beads are not obtainable or beyond the purse of the user, people opt for small rosaries called *bobeekhas*, which generally contain 6,9,12,18,27,36 or 54 beds i.e. any sub-multiple of 108.

Different religious and sects have their own types of rosaries. The Buddhist rosary is probably of b*rahmin* origin and has 108 beads. This is said to correspond with the number of mental conditions or sinful inclinations which are overcome by reciting mantras using the beads. Also, 108 *brahmins* were summoned at Buddha's birth to foretell his destiny. Besides the full rosaries of 108 beads, smaller ones are also used, the number of beads representing the chief disciples of Buddha.

The Jain sect use the sandalwood rosary to repeat the *navakar mantra*. The more affluent ones use beads of red coral, emerald, silver, gold and other precious gems. Different colours have been attributed to the Jain *tirthankaras* – red, yellow green, white and dark. Therefore, rosaries in these five hues are made and used.

The Sikhs have a rosary which consists of knots instead of beads and which is made of many strands of wool, knotted together at intervals – 108 knots in all. Another kind of rosary used by Sikhs is made of iron beads connected by slender iron links.

In Tibet, the rosary is an essential part of the Lama's dress and is also worn by most of the laity of both sexes. The rosary, called *phreng-ba*, has 108 beads. The reason for this number is that it ensures the repetition of the sacred *mantra* 100 times. The eight extra beads being added lest there is omission or breakage. Yet, an extra bead is often strung with those on the main string, bringing the number up to 109. The act of telling the beads in called *tance*, which literally means 'to purr' like a cat – the muttering of the prayers being akin to this sound.

China has the usual number of 108 beads, with 3 dividing beads of a different size or colour. The materials used vary. There are also smaller rosaries of 18 beads, corresponding to the 13 *lohans* (chief disciples of Buddha). In Japan, the Buddhist rosary has a complicated form, each sect having its own. In former times rosaries were made from the wood of the *Bodhi* or Peepul tree, for under its shade, Sakyamuni is said to have attained supreme and universal enlightenment. Due to difficulty of obtaining this wood, common rosaries are made from the wood of the cherry or plum trees.

The rosary used by Muslims, generally consists of 99 beads with a terminal bead called the *imam* or 'leader'. Its chief use is to count the recital of the 99 names or attributes of god, the *imam* being sometimes used for the essential name, *Allah*. For practical daily use, rosaries with 33 beads only are in vogue. According to some authorities, there is another variety of rosary, rarely used, which has 101 beads, tsimilar to the rosary is called *tasbih* in Egypt.

The materials for rosaries range from wood, date stones, horn, camel bones to imitation pearls to corals and gems. Beads made from the clay of Mecca, are highly valued. Another rosary from India, used by Arabs of the Sunni sect, has beads made from the black seeds of the *Gannabis Indica* and are inlaid with silver. Sometimes rosary beads are dyed red in honour of Husain, who was slain by Yazid, the seventh Kalifah – the red representing his blood. Sometimes the beads are green in honour of Easan, who met his death by poisoning which caused his body to turn green. Fakirs on the other hand, prefer coloured glass beads and also amber or agate.

The use of the rosary among Christians was introduced by St. Aybert de Crespin, Peter the Hermit and St. Dominic.

The word 'rosary' has its root in the Latin *rosarium*, meaning 'rose garden'. The rosary used by Catholics consists of 150 *Ave Marias* (prayers to the Virgin Mary) and 15 *Paternosters* (the Lord's Prayer) and *Glorias*. It is a string of 165 beads for keeping count of these prayers linked to the adoration of the Virgin Mary. A pendant is usually attached, consisting of a cross or crucifix and one large and three smaller beads.

In the hands of idols and deities, we often find the rosary, as with the goddess Saraswati. From primitive means of counting his prayers using pebbles or his fingers, Man evolved the sophisticated rosary. The Hindus were the first to start using the rosary or *japamala*, then the Buddhists, the Muslims and finally the Christians learnt to use it.

The rosary is lan article of veneration. After completing the telling of the beads and prayers, obeisance is made to the rosary by touching it to one's forehead and then it is placed kept carefully in a box.

KAJAL ~ COLLYRIUM

Kajal is a cosmetic applied to around the eyes. The black colour enhances the beauty by making the eyes look lustrous and attractive. The custom of applying *kajal* has been prevalent since ancient times. Other names for *kajal* are *anjan* and *surma*.

The process of making *kajal* is given in the *Sushruti* manual. A copper plate is put on a flame lighted by castor oil or clarified butter (*ghee*). This flame forms the black soot called *kajal*.

During the Hindu marriage ceremony, it is customary to apply *kajal* to the eyes of the bride and groom. Again on the fourth day of the marriage, the newly-weds apply *kajal* on each other's eyes, praying to make their eyes bright and rapturous. It is believed that evil spirits and the devil are afraid of the black *kajal* and thus it is applied to the *batu* or novitiate, during his thread ceremony and to the bridal couple at wedding ceremonies. Especially on religious festivals, it is the tradition for *sushasini* (those with husbands who are alive) ladies to apply *kajal*. Before any religious ceremony or auspicious occasion, the *suhasini* lady uses *kajal*. . It is also common practice to apply *kajal* to the eyes of infants and small children to prevent diseases of the eyes and to maintain the eyes in good condition.

There are several varieties of *kajal* – for example *surma*, which is mainly used by the Muslims. Certain varieties of *kajal* cause the eyes to water, thought to thereby cleanse the eyes and make them clear. Legend has it that when Moses had a vision of Allah on Mt Sinai, he fainted and the mountain caught fire, so Allah proclaimed, 'From this day on, all of you shall grind the mud of the earth of this mountain very fine and apply it to your eyes.'

The main significance of *kajal* or *surma* is to ward off evil and protect one from the evil eye. Thus , a black spot of kajal is put on children's cheeks or on any beautiful person, so that no *nazar* or evil eye is cast on them. In many sculptures and frescoes on ancient monuments, we find women depicted with almond eyes, in the act of applying *kajal* to their eyes.

Kajal, anjan or *surma* has been a prime subject in literature. Poems are rife with descriptions of the *kajal* in Lord Krishna's eyes or that of the *gopis* or courtesans. Lovers of art have also extolled the enchanting effect of *kajal* highlighting a woman's eyes.

Kajal is one of the 16 important articles that constitute a woman's shringar or make-up. Kajal, along with kumkum, has been regarded as an auspicious symbol of good luck and fortune for Hindu *suhasini* woman.

KALASH ~ POT

The *kalash* is an essential item in our Hindu religious ceremonies. It is a tall vessel with a round body and broad rim for storing water.

In the legend of the churning of the ocean, when the *amrit* or nectar of immortality, was obtained from the waters, the gods asked Vishvakarma, their architect, to specially create this pot or *kalash,* to hold the nectar.

Before starting any religious ceremony, the *kalash* is filled with water and a stalk of five mango leaves is placed on it. A pinch of vermillion or *kumkum,* turmeric or *haldi* and a sprig of *Tulsi* is put into it and a coconut placed on top of the mango leaves, thus sanctifying the *kalash.* The water represents Lord Varun, god of rain and water. In ancient times, the *rishis* developed the *kalash* as a container to store water during droughts and they worshipped Varun through the *kalash* containing water. Thus the importance of the *kalash* began and every auspicious ceremony now begins with the worship of the *kalash.*

There are nine types of *kalash* as follows: *Kshitindra, Jalasambhav, Pavan, Agni, Yajaman, Koshsambha, Som, Aditya and Vijay.* They are meant to be placed in specific positions in the north, south, east and west, during *pujas.* Parts of the *kalash* have been allotted to different gods. At the mouth is Brahma; at the throat lives Lord Shiva; at the root Vishnu; in the middle the goddesses; surrounding it the *dikpals* (supporters of the regions); and in the belly the Ganges, the four *Vedas,* planets starsetc. (*Kalipuran*). According to some, Vishnu is confined to the mouth and Brahma to the base.

During any auspicious ceremony such as marriage or *puja,* the *kalash* is first installed. During *Gauri puja* at the *Ganapati* festival, the *kalash* is filled with rice and covered with cloth. It is then placed on a banana leaf with rice spread on it. A coconut is coloured white with lime and the beautiful face of the goddess drawn on it and *haldi* and *kumkum* applied. The coconut is then decorated with cloth, ornaments and flowers.

Likewise, during the *vrata* (fast) of *Vara-Lakshmi,* which falls during *Navaratri,* a *swastik* is drawn and some rice or wheat flour spread on it. Then the *kalash* is filled with rice and mango leaves placed on top. A golden image of Lakshmi is put atop the *kalash* which is decorating with sacred cloth, ornaments and flowers.

In Bengal, *Durga puja* starts on the sixth day of *Navaratri,* when the *kalash* is installed, called *ghata sthapana.* The kalash is filled with water or rice and mango leaves and a coconut or *daab* with the *swastika,* is placed on top of it. Only after this is the idol of Durga infused with 'Life', a ceremony known as *pran prathishta* and *drishti daan* i.e. instilling eyesigh – after which, worship of Durga begins.

Rishis use to placea copper *kalash* on the pinnacle of the temple to protect it from lightning and also perhaps to give the *kalash* the highest honour. But they soon found that copper turned black with time, so they enamelled or plated the pot with gold so it would remain bright and be visible to devotees from a long distance away.

Enthroning the gold-plated *kalash* on top of the temple enabled pilgrims to realize its importance and brilliance. In fact, temple construction is considered complete only after placing the *kalash* with a coconut at pinnacle.

In the Buddhist religion too, the *kalash* is an important and five large, sanctified *kalash* symbolizing the five wise disciples of Lord Buddha, are placed on the altar. The *kalash* has remained a utility item as well as a mystic symbol and special sign of reaching knowledge. During the crowning of kings of yore, four *kalash* filled with the water of four oceans, were placed near the king's throne. With the waters of these *kalash,* the king was anointed or *abhishek* was performed. Kalidasa has thus described the *Rajyabhishek* of Lord Ramchandra in one of his books.

Buddhist craftsmen have endowed the *kalash* with their decorative skills, giving it an aesthetic touch. These elements are largely prevalent in Sanchi Amravati and other sites of Buddhist architecture. Hindu craftsmen also created various shaped *kalash* – round, oval, egg-shaped, tall with a narrow tall neck and so on.

Saint Gnyaneshwar, in his commentary on the *Bhagavad Gita,* called the 18th and concluding chapter **Kalashodhya.** The *kalash* is regarded as a symbol of spirituality and holy men were said to store the nectar of their compassion in the *kalash.* *Rishis* of ancient times have compared the *kalash* to the body and the water within it to life. Credit goes to the artisans or potters who, by creating the full *kumbh* or *kalash,* made the allegory real. The sacred leaves in the *kalash* and the five alloys used in its casting, is suggestive of the five elements of the cosmos. In our daily life, the Kalash is used to store water but it is also a religious symbol for attaining salvation. Thus, just as the human body without life is useless, similarly an empty *kalash* in religious ceremonies loses its sanctity and is no more than an ordinary pitcher.

Among the Hindus, when a new bride is welcomed to her new home, a *kalash* filled with rice is placed at the threshold. Before entering, the bride overturns the *kalash* with her foot, spilling the rice, thus symbolizing the bringing in of prosperity and wealth in abundance.

KAMAL ~ LOTUS

*K*amal is the lotus *Nebumbium nelumbo,* a water lily which is sacred specially to the Hindus but also to the Buddhists. It has various other names carrying different implications such as: *Padma, Pushkar, Arvind, Tamras, Rajiv, Ambhuj, Saroj, Pankaj, Punarika* (white lotus), *Kuvalaya* (blue lotus), *Kumuda* and *Manjula.* The female lotus is called *Kamalini.* The lotus grows in various shades of mauve, pink, red as well as blue, cream and white.

The symbolic use of the lotus is various and remarkable. It is said to variously represent, the sun and moon; the attribute of silence; female beauty; the breath of the gods; and the source of the nectar that gives eternal life. Lakshmi, the goddess of wealth, is seen seated upon it, the fragrance of her body filling the heavens. Kamadeva, the Hindu Cupid, floats down the Ganges on this flower. The Japanese Mercury, Fudo, is said to glide through the air on lotus sandals. With the Egyptians it is the flower of Osiris, the sun god; and Horus, son of Osiris and the god of silence, sits on a lotus with a finger to his lips.

From ancient times, the lotus or *kamal* has been a favourite flower of the Hindus. In the *Rig Veda,* there is mention of the lotus as *Pundarik* (white lotus) and *Pushkar* (blue lotus). Indeed, they are also known as the temples of the sea.

A legend about the lotus relates to the origin of the universe and is mentioned in the *Brahmana* scriptures: in the beginning the universe was in a liquid state. When Lord Prajapati was thinking of expansions, he found a lotus leaf in the water. Presuming there must be some ground below, he took the form of a bore and dove deep into the water. He came across earth, a bit of which he grabbed and coming out of the water again, spread it on the lotus leaf and so created land. One of the scriptures even narrates that the birth of Prajapati himself took place on this leaf.

A lotus floating on water is thus the symbol of the world or earth. Brahma the Creator, emerged from a lotus which sprang from Vishnu's navel and from this rostrum commanded all worlds into being. The lotus symbolizes beauty and perfection for according to Brahma, it is the synonym of the goddess Lakshmi. It is also said that the lotus was dyed with the blood of Shiva when it flowed from where Kamadeva's , the Hindu God of Love's arrow injured him.

In the *Atharva Veda*, the heart of a person is known as *pundarik* (white lotus). Ashwini Dev, another god, adorns himself with a garland of blue lotuses. There is a vessel called *pushkar*, in the shape of a lotus, which was used during sacrificial rites.

Lord Buddha is often shown seated sits on an open lotus, resting his feet on another lotus. Buddhists claim that the new-born Buddha, in setting foot on earth, caused a lotus to spring up and that a lotus marked each his first 7 steps. *Om manipadme* (O God, the jewel of the lotus), is a Buddhist prayer or *mantra*.

Mahayana Buddhists imagine a heaven called *sukhavati*, where they maintain that every soul unfolds from a lotus and thrives in a garden of lotuses. Jainism has also revered the lotus and their sculptures in particular use the lotus extensively as a decorative element.

Over 5000 years of Indian cultural history has seen the use of the lotus as a symbol for many auspicious things. In the *Vayupuran*, the shape of the earth has been described to be like a lotus. If there happens to be a lotus mark on a person's arm, then according to palmistry, he is predicted to become a monarch. Moreover, since both Vishnu and Lakshmi adore for lotus, it has attained pride of place and is honoured by Hindus. *Padmapurana* of the Viashnavites, has extolled the lotus highly and the following story is an example.

Once there lived a hunter named Dandapani, who sustained his family by hunting animals and robbing travelers. One day, a *brahmin* wanted a lotus to perform Vishnu *puja*. Unable to find one, he approached the hunter. Dandapani searched and eventually brought him the lotus. By the very act of giving the lotus to the *brahmin*, the hunter was reprieved of all his sins and in his next birth attained the status of a learned *brahmin*. Thus, making a *daan* or a gift of the lotus is said to bring immeasurable merit to the giver.

The lotus thrives in water yet amazingly, not even a drop remains on the lotus or its leaves. Hence, the lotus is thought of as the perfect example of detachment. Also, when extolling gods and goddesses, devotees compare the feet of deities with a lotus or use it as a simile.

The sun is compared to a red lotus emerging from the blue ocean-like sky. At sunrise the lotus blooms and faces the sun and at sunset it closes itself, to blossom again the next morning at sunrise. Similarly, a *yogi* meditates to attain self-realization from morning till sunset and then retires.

Since earliest times the lotus has been used as an emblem and motif of ornamentation in both realistic and conventionalized forms in architecture, textiles, embroidery, pottery and so on.

The lotus has been much alluded to in literature. Also, to draw a *rangoli* or traditional floor design, of the eight-petalled lotus, in the house, is said to bring Lakshmi and hence wealth and prosperity to the family.

In many excavations, images of Lakshmi emerging from a lotus or holding a lotus, have been found. In Mohenjodaro, a figurine of a woman with a lotus flower in her hair, has been found. Many *Pauranik* deities have also been found enthroned on the lotus. In another excavation, an image of Buddha seated on a large lotus with his devotees surrounding him at his feet, has been unearthed.

In architecture too, Hindu, Buddhist and Jain temples have carvings of the lotus on their domes and walls. Muslim rulers used the lotus in their architecture too, perhaps owing to the Hindu spiritual influence. The dome of the Taj Mahal resembles an inverted lotus resting on its petals.

Being simple, decorative and attractive, the lotus lends itself to columns, paintings, wall ornaments and also the carpets of Turkey and Persia. It must have been first regarded merely for its beauty and painters and sculptors used it without any thought of symbolism. But, when its petals suggested the rays of the sun, it must have entered into sun worship. The lotus was a sacred flower in Egypt 4,000 years ago, and was used to decorate guests at banquets, the stem being wound about the head and the bud hanging over the forehead. The Japanese still make ceremonial use of the lotus, which they buy on holidays for temple decoration and use its leaves or pods to wrap food that is offered to the dead. In Thailand, where the lotus is the national flower, heaven is suggested though the great lotus ponds in the king's palace near Bangkok. Despite the sanctity of the lotus, the Egyptians, Chinese, Indians and others, eat the bread made from its kernels as well as various preparations from its roots, stems and flowers. The roots, in particular, are said to contain medicinal properties.

The lotus is prominent in the *Yoga Shashtra*, where the six *chakras* of the body are depicted with the lotus as the base. In the human body, life and strength are said to flow from head to toe, but in spiritual terms, the *kundalini* rises from under the spinal cord and travels upwards, crossing the lotus-based *chakras* to reach *sahasrar*. In yoga practice, one of the *asanas*, is known as *Padmasana* or the lotus posture.

The lotus is also cultivated in many parts of India. At one time, the Dal Lake in Srinagar, Kashmir, used to be completely covered with pink lotuses and their large green leaves.

KARPUR ~ CAMPHOR

One of the items always used in Hindu ritual worship is camphor or as it is commonly called, *karpur*. The origin of camphor can he traced to a large evergreen tree, the *Cinnamomum camphora*. It is an aromatic tree with dense foliage and is classified in the family *Lauraceae* (laurel). It grows to 40 feet (12 metres) and has shiny thick leaves, small yellow flowers and berry-like fruits.

The camphor tree is cultivated in the Nilgiris in south India and also in some parts of the north. This evergreen tree is a native of China and Japan and is often planted for ornamentation, specially along roads in Texas, southern California and Florida, where it also grows in the wild.

The juices of the tree contain camphor, which is obtained by steam distillation of the wood and the leaves. There are other sources of camphor too, for example, from certain species of *ocimum* and the genus of the *Tulsi* plant. Camphor can also be obtained from the root, bark and oil of the cinnamon tree by allowing the oil to stand for some time so that the camphor separates.

Camphor is said to be translucent, aromatic and highly volatile. From ancient times it has been important in ritual worship. While performing *aarti* to the deities, camphor pieces are used instead of wicks. Again, especially for *havans*, chunks of camphor keep the fire going as camphor ignites easily. It has a strong fragrant vapour which is said to purify the air. It is believed that the deities are fond of this smell while evil spirits dislike it. Hence it wards off evil elements or spirits. Camphor is thus considered sacred.

Because of its fragrance, camphor is treated and used as a flavouring agent in sweets and confectionary. It is also used to purify drinking water. Camphor has great medicinal value and is used in balms and liniments as a counter irritant because of its powerful smell. As a home remedy for rheumatism, muscular pain, stiff joints, lumbago etc., a few grains of camphor dissolved in mustard oil and kept in the sun, proves to be an effective liniment. Camphor is also used as an anesthetic and mild antiseptic for skin complaints. Camphor is extremely beneficial in respiratory ailments. Orally, it serves as a circulatory stimulant and expectorant, thus getting rid of phlegm and bringing relief to people suffering from chest colds and bronchitis. Dissolved in plain oil, and used as a nasal paint, it is effective in common colds too. It is also said to stimulate and strengthen the heart.

Commercially it is used as a preservative in drugs and cosmetics and also in the manufacture of plastics. One can make an aromatic satchet with dried and crushed camphor leaves and keep it amidst one's clothes as a moth-repellant.

Camphor, although regarded as sacred, serves many others useful purposes.

KUMKUM or SINDUR ~ VERMILLION

*K*umkum or vermillion, is a sign of great auspiciousness in the Hindu religion. Every Hindu married woman applies *kumkum* on her forehead or to the parting of her hair. It denotes her married state and that her husband is alive.

In *Vedic* times, usage of *kumkum* did not exist. It was only after the *Upanishadic* period that it came into use. During the age of the epic *Mahabharata*, mention of *kumkum* is made. It is thought that *kumkum* came into prominence in the 3rd or 4th century AD.

Kumkum, also known as *sindur*, is made from red oxide. Actually, *kumkum* in its pure form, is made from a combination of *alum* and *turmeric* which have disinfectant properties and give the red colour. In present times, other chemical elements are mixed to make it bright or indeed to give it other colours, to match the ladies' fashion-wear.

In all Hindu religious ceremonies, the use of *kumkum* and *haldi* (turmeric) are considered essential. While performing *puja*, the images of gods and goddesses are applied with both *haldi* and *kumkum*. During festivals, functions are held where ladies are specially invited and offered *haldi- kumkum*. Young girls and married woman with living husbands, had the privilege of using *kumkum*. The absence of *kumkum* or a *bindi* signified widowhood.

The custom of applying *kumkum* was picked up by the Aryans from the non-Aryan population. During the Gupta Age, many non-Aryans became involved with the customs of the *Pauranik* religion. An exchange of cultural and religious customs resulted. During this period, many non-Aryan and Dravidian gods got absorbed into the Aryan religion. In this process, Aryan women accepted the non-Aryan *kumkum* as the symbol of *saubhagyavathi* (a woman who is blessed).

The colour of *kumkum* being red, is both intriguing and of great importance. In early matriarchal times, the colour red was given great importance as it was said to be loved by the gods. Furthermore, the use of *kumkum* was associated with animal sacrifice. In the *Shakta* religious services, animal blood was applied to the forehead of the Goddess. A woman is considered to be the embodiment of Goddess Jagadamba, the incarnation of Shakti. Hence, in former times, when a bride in south India was first welcomed into her new home as *Grihalakshmi*, the blood of an animal was applied as *tilak* to the bride's forehead. Only then did she enter the house. This custom is prevalent even today among the *Adivasi* tribes and in an amended manner using *kumkum* as an auspicious symbol, in modern households.

When donning a new *saree*, many Hindu women first place a dot of *kumkum* on the new *saree*. During Diwali, on the occasion of *Bhavubij, kumkum* is applied to a brother's forehead by his sister. The auspiciousness of *kumkum* is such that it is applied even on wedding cards before they are distributed

In the Hindu marriage ceremony, the groom applies *sindur* in the parting of the bride's hair. *Kumkum* is applied to both bride and groom in the course of the ceremony and this is also a custom prevalent among the Parsis. When a Hindu bride first enters her husband's house, she first steps into a *thali* or platter filled with water and vermillion at the entrance. As she walks in, she leaves vermillion footprints, symbolizing the entry of the Godess Lakshmi into the house. Moreover, when anybody is leaving his home on an auspicious mission, water with *kumkum* is waved before him to ward off evil as well as for protection.

In olden days, young girls placed a dot of *kumkum* on their foreheads and elderly women used a horizontal shape. Women of the *Shaivite* sect applied it in a crescent while *Vaishnavite* women used the round moon shape. In the north and east of India, especially among Bengalis, *sindoor* is spread in the parting of the hair.

Rishis claimed that the bridge of the nose, the meeting point of the eye-brows, was the most sensitive part of the body. They averred that this spot was the *agya-chakra* or wheel of wisdom and that this vulnerable point was to be kept warm and protected. The *rishis* Charak and Sushruta explained that the forehead, forearms and temples, were the best for beneficial as well as decorative purposes. In modern times many women do not give importance to the *bindi* or to wearing *sindur*. But one heartening aspect today is that widows too are encouraged to use *bindis* and *kumkum*, which was once considered sacrilegious.

MANGAL SUTRA ~
AUSPICIOUS CORD OF MATRIMONY

In a Hindu marriage ceremony the *mangal sutra* plays an important part but in *Vedic* times it did not exist. It was introduced later from the Dravidian culture of the south. It is presumed that the ritual of tying the *tali* (the ornamental symbol of auspiciousness and *suhagan* or matrimony), on the bride, in Tamil Nadu, must have been picked up as the *mangal sutra* of today.

The *mangal sutra* is a necklace of black beads which are strung on two thin gold cords with a pendant called *tali* or *bottu*. Small beads of gold are placed in between the black to enhance the beauty of the ornament and are designed in various ways.

It is customary for the parents of the bride to provide the *mangal sutra*. *Mangal* signifies anything auspicious and *sutra* means the cord or thread on which the black beads are strung. The black beads are used because black is supposed to ward off any evil. The *mangal sutra* corresponds to the Christian wedding ring which in fact originated in pagan culture.

During the Hindu marriage ceremony, there is a ritual called the *kankana bandhan*, when the bridal couple tie a thread with a turmeric piece attached, on each other's wrists and mark their forhead with the *tilak*. This is followed by the tying the *mangal sutra* by the groom round the neck of the bride, speaking the mantra: *This string is the string of my life. I am tying this around thy neck. May I live long, O blessed one, may thou too live a hundred autumns.* But, before tying it on, the *mangal sutra* is passed round to be blessed by the wedding guests, specially elderly *suhagan* ladies (with living husbands). The bride then wears it as long as her husband is alive. If she becomes a widow, she no longer wears it, just as she does not use *sindur*. It obviously signifies the substitution of the *sati* rites of the past. Just as men without the sacred thread did not perform any religious ceremonies, widows did not participate in any religious functions or perform them.

In some communities, a string stained with *haldi* or turmeric, is substituted for the *mangal sutra* and *tali*. In northern India, the custom of the *mangal sutra* is not prevalent. Intsead, bangles are given more importance and considered symbols of marriage, besides *sindur*, and when a women is windowed she breaks or removes her bangles.
Young girls adorn themselves with multicolored bangles and apply *haldi-kumkum* but a *mangal-sutra* is worn only by *suhagan* women.

In some communities in Maharshtra and Karnataka, the bride wears the *mangal sutra* for one year with the *tali* inverted. After a year, the *mangal sutra* is worn with the *tali* facing the right side up.

Again, there is a necklace called *adit dora* worn by some Brahmin women. It is made of a tube of gold about an inch long. On each side of this mystic tube, are placed beads of gold. The rest of the necklace is made up of minute gold or glass beads. This necklace is worn only by *suhagan* women and is worshiped on Sundays in the month of *Shravan*.

Thus the *mangal sutra* is considered the most auspicious ornament of a married woman and is never removed in her husband's lifetime because of its sacred and symbolic value. Any other necklaces and adornments are worn additionally.

MANJIRA or KAFI ~ CYMBALS

Cymbals, are a percussion instrument of great antiquity, comprising of two concave plates of brass or bronze that produce sharp ringing sound when struck together. The metal plates are of indefinite pitch and are either used in pairs, that is two cymbals being struck together or singly, sounded with a beater or mallet generally made of metal or wood while some are covered with felt or yarn.

Cymbals are known by many different names even within India – the small ones used in devotionals are called *manjira* and the large cymbals are known as *kafi*. Other names used are *jhanj, tala, khanjani* etc.

The centre of a cymbal resembles the crown of a hat. A musician can hold the cymbal by means of a leather handle attached to its centre or hang the instrument on a stand, much like a hat.

In the great Oriental religions, particularly Hinduism and Buddhism, cymbals, like drums, have an important place in temple worship. Cymbals were known in early India and are still used by Hindus at home and in temples as an accompaniment while singing devotional songs. Small cymbals with cords tied to keep them together, are used for rhythm by performers of *kirtans* (musical narration), and large ones called *zariga*, are used to perform *aarti*. Saints like Chaitanya Mahaprabhu, Ramprosad and others, are depicted with *khanjanis* or small cymbals which are used to keep rhythm while singing devotional songs.

In Buddhist temples, huge cymbals of vast diameter, are used. In Bundelkhand, a unique type of cymbal called *chital*, made from two long iron plates, one side pointed and sharp and the other side fixed in a chain or linked, is used. The Garos from the northeast of India, use two sorts of cymbals – the *kakwa* like the European or Greco-Roman and the *nengilsi*, or smaller kind resembling two small brass cups.

Cymbals were found in the excavations of the Indus Valley, a civilization which existed about 2,500 BC. Deemed to have originated in Asia, cymbals spread throughout the ancient Orient and to medieval Europe where they served as ceremonial instruments. As purveyors of oriental music, cymbals were first used in opera towards the end of the 17th century. Later, along with other prominent features of the highly developed Turkish bands of the period, cymbals gradually lost their Oriental connotation and became standard percussion instruments in modern orchestras and bands. Cymbals came to be introduced in Military Music too. Very small antique cymbals or *crotales,* with a high but definite pitch, are used in orchestral scores, as in the music of Debussy and Stockhausen. Free-standing cymbals are also an important part of the jazz drummer's kit. The Turkish or 'buzz' cymbals, incorporate loose rivets to extend the sound.

Cymbals range from 2-40 inches in diameter. Most musicians prefer cymbals that measure between 30-35 centimeters in diameter. They also vary in thickness and no two sounds are exactly alike. The Zildijian Company in the United States, manufacture the most widely used cymbals in the world. They have been making cymbals using their own secret method, since 1623. The company originated in Turkey and *zildjian* is the Turkish word for cymbals.

OM or AUM ~ SACRED SOUND

O m is the most sacred *mantra* of Hinduism. An alternate transliteration of *Aum* (the sounds A and U blend to become *Om*) is, according to *Encyclopedia of India*, 'a mystic monosyllable and sacred explanation, the object of profound religious mediation and reverence throughout Hindu India, taken to symbolize all sound and reality'.

Om comprises three independent letters A, U, M. 'A' represents the beginning (*adi-matva*), 'U' represents progress (*utkarsha*), 'M' represents limit or dissolution (*miti*). Hence, *Om* represents the power responsible for creation, development and dissolution of this Universe or God himself.

Om is also referred to as *pranava* and is the universally accepted symbol of Hinduism which has been extolled in the *Vedas*, the *Upanishads* and the *Gita*. *Om* is the *vedic* symbol of the Supreme Being. The magic potency of *Om* (*Aum*), whose very letters a, u and m are held represent the first three *Vedas*, signifies the theistic triad of Brahma, Vishnu and Shiva (Creator, Preserver, Annihilator).

Swami Vivekananda, in one of his lectures, explains that there must be a natural connection between a symbol and what it identifies, thus it recalls the thing signified. He avers that the manifesting word of God is *Om*. There are hundreds of words for God or the idea of a Supreme Being, But representing them all is *Om*.

Swami Vivekananda also observes that in terms of phonetics, *Om* is the basis of all sounds. The most natural sound which manifests all other sounds is *Om (Aum)*. The syllable *Om*, is constituted of three letters – the first, 'A' (pronounce 'all'), is the root or key sound, pronounced without touching any part of the tongue to the palate; 'M' represents the last sound in the series (pronounced 'ma' as in 'maul') through closed lips; and the U (pronounced as in 'put'), rolls from the very root to the end of the sounding board of the mouth, each with a meaning, is the most comprehensive of all verbal symbols. Thus, *Om* represents the whole phenomena of sound and is the natural symbol, and matrix of all sounds.

Om has become the one symbol for religious aspiration of the vast majority of human beings. Swami Vivekananda goes further to say that while with the words for God in many other language, covers a limited function and hence significance, *Om* combines all aspects, wherein lies its greatness and importance.

Meditation on the attributes of *brahman* usually takes the form of meditation on the sacred syllable *Om* referred to as *pranava*. Gaudapada, the illustrious predecessor of Sankara, in one of his commentaries on the *Mandukya Upanishad,* has expounded that *Om* is the sound which is indicative of *Brahman*. So, for purposes of meditation, *Om* is used to stand for the Self or *Brahman*.

Swami Ram Tirtha, writing about *Om* says, 'In the *mantram Om (Aum)*, the first letter 'A' stands for this stern Reality, your self, as underlying and manifesting the illusory material world of the wakeful state. 'U' represents the Psychic word. And the last letter 'M' denotes the Absolute Self as underlying the chaotic state and manifesting itself as al the unknown.'

He goes to say that in *Aum,* 'A' 'U' and 'M' are sometimes called *matras* or forms but that *Om* does not stop at *matra* or for it stands for the reality, underlies all *matras.* Reality or true life, is our own Self, the *atman* which is represented by *Om.* It thus means the Reality behind the scenes, the eternal Truth and the indestructible Self that we all are.

Mediation on *Om* is well recognized in the *Upanishads.* The *Mandukya Upanishad,* expounding the significance of *omkara,* sketches the method of identifying the components of the sound *Om* with aspects of Self – thereby realizing the truth of non-duality. There are four *matras* or *morae* of *Om* corresponding to the four phases of the Self – a, u,m and the fourth is represented by the point (*bindu*) of the *anusvara.* The phases of the Self are *Visva, Taijaa, Prajna* and the *Turiya* – the first three stand for the Self in waking, dream and sleep states respectively, and the fourth is the Self *per se.* The principle of meditation on *Om* is to equate the *matras* with the phases and this equation or knowledge is called *matrasampratipatti* (i.e. knowing the matras to be identical with the phases) and *omkarasyapandasovidya* (knowledge of the *morae* of *Om* as the phases of the Self).

All the *Vedas,* Vedanta and other sacred scriptures of the Hindus, are known to be contain Om but it is a sacred syllable in other religions too, as with the Hebrews in Judaism, in Islam, and Christians end their prayers with 'Amen'. Jainism and Buddhists have also absorbed this sacred syllable as in their holy *mantra, Om Manipadme Hum,* which begins with *omkar.* Buddhist philosophy claims *Om* to have originated from *shunya* or zero and the creation of the cosmos.

According to Max Mueller, *Om* came into existence from the root form *av* which later became *avam,* then evolved into *aum* and finally blend into *Om.*

Panini's definition is that *Omkar* existed from the beginning and there was no transition of shorter or long vowels of A to make *Aum*. In course of time, during the period of the *Brahmanas* and the *Upanishads*, mysticism became involved with the syllable *Om*. Thus the *Aitreya Brahamana* states the three letters AUM have arisen from *bhur bhuv svah*. In the *Taitreys Upanishad*, *Om* is identified as Brahma and the creation, progress and dissolution of the Universe are believed to happen with its aid.

Amongs the many explanations which exist regarding the origin of *Om*, Durgadas, the grammarian, states that *Omkar* had emerged from the throat of Brahmadev and is thus considered very auspicious. Manu too, emphasized that *Om* should be uttered before and at the end of any recitation of *vedic mantras*. In Indian philosophical doctrines, *Om* has been regarded as the means of attaining self realization. Patanjali in his *Yogasutra*, has recommended this *pranav* be fused into our lives.

In *puranic* literature there is mention of how different sects interpreted *Om* in their own way. In *Shivapuran*, *Omkar* has been regarded as the symbol of *Panchmukh Shiva* (five-faced Shiva). In *Vishnupuran*, the *Om (Aum)* is regarded as the symbol of Vishnu. *Om* or *pranava* have been understood to mean the three *Vedas*, the three worlds, and Lord Vishnu's three strides. The *Gita* mentions that *Om Tatsat*, the Absolute, has been defined in the *Shastras* or scriptures as being of three types (Brahman, Ved and Sacrifice). Hence, sacrifice, penance, giftingand other rituals, always commence with the syllable *Om* or *Aum*.

Om chanting has many benefits and serves as the medium of unity between the Individual Self and the Supreme Self. Through deep meditation on Om, the Self becomes unified with the *brahman* and all things merges into one.

According to theories of *yoga*, while chanting *Om* the vibrations reach the organs, tissues, nerve cells and endocrine glands, resulting in better functioning of the body and mind. It improves respiration. The vibrations fill the entire field of consciousness, the intensity of thought becoming less and less. Gradually, with practice, the chanter experiences complete recession of thought, bringing peace and calm to the mind and increasing concentration. Finally, all stress and tensions are removed, so that the body and mind enter a state of complete relaxation.

According to modern research, *Om* chanting clears the sinuses and wards off infections. Chanting is said to create sound vibrations which encourage air to move back and forth between our sinus membranes and nasal passages.

Swami Ram Tirtha reiterates that the worst enemy we have is our own self, and that while chanting *Om* we should work our minds to the realization of all that is negative and root it out along with thoughts of separateness from our Supreme Self.

Gaudapada, while concluding his exposition on *Pranava Yoga* remarks, '*Om* is to be known as the Lord present in the heart of all. Having understood the all-pervading *Om* the wise one does not grieve about anything. *Omkara* is without measure (*amastra*), and is without limits (*ananta-matra*). It is That in which all duality ceases, it is Bliss. He who knows this is a saint, and no other.'

The *Kathopanisad* says, 'The word(or goal) which all the *Vedas* declare, that which penances proclaim, and desiring which people lead an austere life, that word (or goal) I tell thee in brief. It is *Om.*' The *Mundakopanisad* compares *Om* to the bow, the individual soul to the arrow, and *Brahman* to the target. When the target is hit, union with *Brahman* attained.

PAAN ~ BETEL LEAF

The name of the Betel vine, Piper Betel, is derived via the Portuguese, from the Malayalam or Tamil *vettile*. The practice of Betel nut (*supari*) and Betel leaf (*paan*) chewing is widespread in India and the South Seas.

It is interesting to see how skilfully *paan* is prepared. The fresh leaf is layered with lime, sprinkled with small pieces of areca nut and other tasty ingredients as required The leaf is then folded over and pinned with a clove and the whole stuffed into the mouth and chewed. The mouth become turns a brilliant red. The areca nut is also called, by transference, the Betel nut and is slightly astringent. It causes mild intoxication, a feeling of euphoria and contentment.

Although universal in India today, the chewing of *paan* was long regarded as a *sudra* (lower caste) custom. There is no mention of it in the *Vedas* or *Sutras* and is first referred to in the *Jataka* tales, an indication that it was derived from a practice current among indigenous tribes.

According to the *Skanda Puran*, the Betel leaf was obtained from the churning of the ocean. The *Mahabharata* narrates that after the victory over the demons, when the *Rajsuya Yagnya* was to be performed, the sages asked for Betel leaves to begin the *yagna*. But, as it was not available anywhere, Arjun had to go to *Nag Lok*, the kingdom of snakes, to procure it from Queen Vasuki Nag. To oblige Arjun, the queen gave him the phalange of her little finger and advised him to sow it and a creeper with leaves would grow. Since the seed of this creeper was a human finger, it is not blessed with flowers or fruits. And since this paan-creeper was acquired the snake queen, it is also called *Nag-Valli* or *Nagarbel*. Mention of the Betel leaf is found in some form or the other in the epics *Ramayana* and *Mahabharata*, as also Buddhist and Jain scriptures. For instance, in the *Mahabharata*, when Vidur visited Lord Krishna, he was offered dinner and excellent *paan*.

Paan has been a link between the Aryans who ruled north India, and the Dravidians who ruled the south. Legend has it that Prince Udayan, son of Surigawati, saw the *paan* leaves for the first time in the *ashram* of Jamadagni, where his mother had taken shelter, in the region ruled by the Naga kings. Fascinated by the creeper, Prince Udayan asked the Naga king for it as a souvenir. Both the Sanskrit words *tambula* (the rolled betel leaf) and *guvaka* (Areca palm), suggest their origin from the south.

Both *paan* and *supari* have a honoured place in our religious ceremonies. The offering of *paan-supari* to the gods, is a significant feature of ceremonial worship. In marriage ceremonies, *paan-supari* is offered to the elders and their blessings sought by the wedded couple. Similarly, offering *paan-supari* to guests is a standard form of hospitality in Hindu as well as Muslim homes. Traditionally, all feasts are rounded off with the delectable *paan*.

In medieval times, the offering of *paan* was attended by elaborate etiquette. 'Bearer of the Betel Bag' was an important functionary in the royal courts, being both purveyor of this

84

pleasurable item and also a kind of physician. Wherever kings went, they were always accompanied by the Betel Bearer and during battles these attendants were often young women who would squat beside the king and periodically pop a prepared Betel leaf into the royal mouth.

There used to be special *paan* gardens termed *bara* (or *bada*), which were enclosures reserved for the rich elite. The extensive grounds in which the harems of the palace women were situated, always contained such an enclosure where the king relaxed with his female entourage, enjoying his *paan*. Interestingly, lovers often used Betel leaves as a special language to convey their secrets thoughts.

There are many varieties of *paan* but according to *Ayurveda*, only two varieties of Betel leaf are edible – the light and the dark varieties. While the dark variety is said to be constipative, the light one is credited with eliminating coughs and being a digestive.

Many things are often added to the basic *pan-supari*. For example, opium to induce sleep, camphor to cool the body. Other components were used to increase sexual prowess, to relieve constipation, to cure diarrhoea, to soothe the nerves etc. It is considered an excellent means for voice development. In India, singers habitually chew *paan*. It is also a breath sweetner. But in contrast to the rich, poor people eat *paan* to stave off hunger pangs because of its narcotic content. In many places, an exchange of paan seals a pact and constitutes a binding oath.

The Betel vine is indigenous to the forests of north-eastern and southern India. It grows easily in the Indian archipelago but in the Indian peninsula, it requires fertilization and care to flourish. The Karens plant the vines in their uplands where there are tall forest trees. The branches of the trees are chopped off, leaving only the topmost boughs with the vines climbing to the top – this method transfoms the whole area into beautiful Betel vine farms. Karens boys compete with each other to see who are the most agile climbers of the *Poo-lab* or Betel trees, in order to impress the unmarried girls.

RUDRAKSH ~ SACRED SEED OF SHIVA

Rudraksh is the seed obtained from the tree *Elecocarpus ganitrus*, found in many parts of India. In the Punjab, however, the name of the *rudraksh* is applied to the seeds of the *Jujubi* tree.

Rudraksh is considered to be the favorite bead of the *Shaivites* and they give as much important to it as to the sacred ash, *vibhuti*. The word *rudraksh* is derived by joining the words *rudra* and *aksha* meaning Shiva's third eye. Since the third eye is considered to be a symbol of great spiritual power, the *rudraksh* is held in the highest esteem.

The *rudraksh* is round with cellular demarcations and a central bore. Small or unmatured bores are also seen but the seed that has only one cellular mark, becomes a piece of great sanctity. The cellular markings or divisions vary from one to twenty-one per seed. Observations by ancient *rishis* or sages, revealed that every seed was a ball of energy and though the efficacy differed between the pieces with different cellular markings, there was no difference in any two identical seeds.

Because of its properties in attracting healthy vibrations, the *rishis* accorded the *rudrakash* a place of high honour in *vedic* and *puranic* times.

Thus the importance of a *rudraksh* is dictated by the number of facets on the seed. These slits, running from end to end, are called *mukh* or mouths. A one-mouthed *rudrakash* is considered a very valuable amulet and the owner of such a bead is said to always have the blessing of the Goddess Lakshmi and enjoy constant prosperity. Further, no weapons could harm the person wearing this amulet.

Rudraksh seeds with 11 facets are worn by celibate *yogis*, while the married ones wear those with only two. The most common and easily available are the five-faceted ones which are sacred to Hanuman, the Monkey God. Due to its sanctity, saints and sages wear necklaces made of *rudraksh*.

The *rudraksh* is considered to be the special ornament of Lord Shiva. The rough surface of the *rudraksh* seeds may possibly symbolize the austerities connected with Shiva worship. According to legend, the seeds are said to be the tears of Rudra (or Shiva) which fell when he was in a rage or grief while killing the demon Tripurasura The tears crystallized into rudraksh beads. The five distinct facets are also thought to stand for five aspects of God.

According to the *Devi Bhagvat*, a *rudraksh* in the shape and size of an *avala* (*emblica microbial*), is considered the most ideal. The rudraksh in the size and shape of the *Jujubi* fruit, is considered of medium or standard value. But a *rudraksh* the size and shape of a pea, is considered inferior.

The cellular markings or facets (*mukhs*), are considered to be symbols of different gods. For example, the 1-*mukhi rudraksh* is said to be favorite of Lord Shiva; the 2-*mukhi* is associated with Shiva and his *shakti*; the 3-*mukhi* is the symbol of Agni; the 4–*mukhi* of Brahmadev; the 5-*mukhi* of Kalagni Rudra; the

6-*mukhi* of Kartik; the 7-*mukhi* of Adisesh; the 8-*mukhi* of Lord Ganesh; the 9-*mukhi* of Bhairav; the 10-*mukhi* of Lord Vishnu; the 11-*mukhi* of Ekadasharudra; the 12-*mukhi* of Lord Surya; the 13-*mukhi* of Kamdev and the 14-*mukhi* of Shiva once again.

Rudraksh are found in four colours – white, red, yellow and black. White and red are considered superior whereas black is regarded as inferior. White and yellow *rudraksh* are rare. Red and black *rudrakash* are more common.

According to the *Tantra Shastra*, a *rudraksh* rosary is extremely beneficial. *Yogis* and Shaivites especially, wear garlands of *rudraksh*. A garland of 27 or 32 beads is worn on the neck; one of 40 beads is worn on the head; one of 6 beads on the ears; one of 12 beads is worn tight round the nape and a garland of 12 beads adorns the staff of a Shaivite. For the actual telling of beads and prayer, a rosary of 108 beads is used.

Rudraksh with *panch-mukhi* or five facets are specially used. While making a *rudraksh* garland, every *mukh* has to be joined to the next *rudraksh*. The terminating main bead of the Rosary, is raised and tied to differentiate it.

Rudraksh has been of great use in *Ayurvedic* medicine. It is believed that if a person wears a *rudraksh* garland, his health stays stable and blood pressure remains normal. Again, its energy charge is said to help and strengthen the heart and reduce tension. Just as a doctor uses a stethoscope to examine a patient, enlightened saints uses the *rudraksh* to read the personality and fortune of their disciples. It is said to determine the positive or negative energy flowing through the body at any time.

A real *rudraksh* is said to be solid in construction so it sinks in a bowl of water. A fake piece will float. There are other scientific means to test the purity of a *rudraksh*. Its aromatic property, helps devotees to go into deep mediation.

According to *Ayurveda*, a *rudraksh* is said to be sour as well as hot and to quench thirst if a minute quantity of its paste is mixed with milk and drunk. Sages advise putting one or two seeds into a silver or copper pot of water and then to sip that water whenever thirsty in order to keep blood pressure under control. A single seed retains its efficacy for about a month.

It is also believed that lightning does not strike the wearer; protects him from accidents; and bestows good luck and fortune. Persons with positive energy currents should wear the rudrakh on the right hand. Those with negative currents have better results on the left hand. Generally speaking, people wearing the *rudraksh* are held in high esteem.

SALAGRAMA ~ STONE OF VISHNU

The *salagrama* is a black ammonite stone found in Nepal, in the river Gandaki, a northern tributary of the Ganges. It is a sort of fossilized shell, oval in shape, with abrasions or tree-like markings on it. It is considered sacred and is usually identified with the god Vishnu or Lord Krishna. Because of its natural mystical markings, it is categorized as *svayambhu* or self-existent.

In the Gandaki mountain, there are insects which perforate the stones and when these perforated stones fall into the river, they are extracted with the use of nets. The stones vary in size and according to size, hollowness, tree-like markings, whorls and different inside colouring and symbols, their price is fixed. At times a thin golden line is also found on them. Depending on their peculiar characteristics, the rarer ones cost as high as tens of thousands of rupees. The more mystic tree-like markings apparent on the *salagrama*, the more highly revered it is.

The *salagramas* are of various colours and according to it the stones are variously named. For example: Shubra.... *Vasudeva;*

Blue......*Hiranyangarbha*; Black....*Vishnu*; Red....*Pradhyumna*; Dark green.....***Srinarayan***; Dark blue......***Narsimha*** or ***Vaman***; the one having twelve *chakras* or wheels, is regarded as ***Anant***. There are 89 kinds of *salagramas* altogether.

It is a common belief that the possessor of one of these, and a shell called *dakshinavarta* (i.e. a shell whose convolutions are towards the right), can never be poor. Generally, the *salagrama* is worshipped in every Vaishnav household where it is reverently bathed and offerings of incense and flowers are presented to it. The *salagramas* are handed down from father to son and are regarded precious heirlooms which must never pass out of the family. It is also believed that parting with them invites misfortune. Hence, few people wish to dispose of them. To sell them for gain is considered to be a most dishonorable deed.

In many Vishnu temples of south India, one finds a garland of *salagramas* on the idol of Vishnu. Though the *salagrama* is looked upon as one of the metamorphoses of Vishnu, the essence of all other deities are also supposed to be present in it and hence *puja* can be offered to other deities through it as well. Brahmins usually worship Vishnu in the form of the *salagrama* by suspending a vessel over it and letting the water drip onto container is placed beneath it to collect the water from sliding off the *salagrama* and this water is drunk by worshippers in the evenings as holy water, to invoke Vishnu. The interstices and the markings on the *salagramas* are shown to dying men in the belief that this will ensure their reaching Vishnu's heaven.

Followers of the Vaishnavite sect revere the *salagramas* more than the image of Lord Vishnu himself. In *Panchayatan* (of five deities) *Puja* also, the *salagrama* is present as the representative of Vishnu. The *salagrama* is said to contain all the *puja* items of the world put together. Even if by some unlucky chance it cracks, it is still held to be worthy of *puja*. The Bairagis are especially particular about *salagramas*. They do not eat without first worshipping it and while doing so, they cover their heads with a piece of cloth upon which the name of Vishnu is inscribed.

The *salagrama* has several legends attached to it. One such story relates that the *salagrama* is identified with Vishnu or Krishna and regarded holy on account of its whorls or interstices which Vishnu, in the form of a worm, is said to have made on its surface.

There is another legend which narrates that Lord Vishnu created the *navagrahas* and assigned them control over the right and wrongs doings of men. As soon as Shani received this power, he went to Brahma and wanted him to be his subject. Brahma, however, referred him to Vishnu. Vishnu, at the sight of Shani, asked Shani to call on him the next day. When Shani called on Vishnu the next day, to his surprise, Vishnu had absconded. So Shani went in search of him, only to find that Vishnu had transformed himself into a mountain near the Gandaki river.

In order to teach Vishnu a lesson, Shani became a worm named Vajrakita and entered the mountain and afflicted Vishnu for 12 years. Vishnu could no longer bear the affliction and two streams of perspiration began to flow from his body. These became the rivers known as Krishna Gandaki and White Gandaki. At the end of 12 years, Vishnu was freed from the influence of Shani. He resumed his proper shape and proclaimed that the stones of the Gandaki mountain be known as *salagramas* and be worshipped as representatives of himself.

Another popular legend is about Tulsi, the plant *Ocimum sanctum*, who, in her former birth was Vrinda, the daughter of a giant named Nemi. She was married to the demon Jalandhar, so called because he was born in water or *jal*. He was born of the sweat which Shiva and thrown off from his brow into the ocean when he perspired at being insulted by Indra. Being born in the ocean, Jalandhar claimed as his heritage the 14 treasures churned out of the ocean. Indra refused to part with them but Jalandhar worshipped Brahma and was blessed with the boon of freedom from death as long as his wife was chaste. Jalandhar fearlessly looted even Amravati, the capital of heaven.

Finally, Vishnu to end his prowess, disguised himself as Jalandhar and deceived Vrinda. Instantly, Jalandhar was killed and Vrinda, realizing the truth, cursed Vishnu into becoming the black *salagrama* stone. In retaliation, Vishnu cursed Vrinda that she would become the shrub *Tulsi*. That is why the *salagrama* is regarded as the symbol of Vishnu. But, even today, in the month of *Kartik*, a mock marriage takes place between the *Tulsi* plant and Vishnu, in the form of the *salagrama*. Veneration of the *salagrama* predates the Aryans and was adroitly adapted to the Hindu religion. The black ammonite stone, the emblem of Vishnu, is however, never installed in temples but only in homes, where it is worshipped and passed down through generations.

SHANKH ~ CONCH

The *shankh* or conch, is an item which is always found in temples and in places of worship, placed before the deities. It is held in reverence because of its religious and mythological associations.

The *shankh* is the shell of the *Turbinella pyrum*. As it plays a prominent role in our religious ceremonies, it is regarded as sacred. Before and during any auspicious function, the *shankh* is blown. As per Hindu mythology, the *shankh* was one of the 14 treasures churned out of the ocean by the *devas* (gods) and the *asuras* (demons). The *shankh* is regarded as the brother of Lakshmi, the goddess of wealth, because both came from the churning of the ocean.

The *shankh* is of natural origin and is said to possess potent powers. When blown with full force, it produces a sonorous and grave tone that fills the air. Thus, in the past, royal proclamations were made by first blowing the *shankh*. During times of war, the *shankh* was blown to commence and end the day's battle and also to inspire and invigorate the armies. Each warrior had a special name for his conch, like Arjuna's

Devdatta; Bhima's *Poundra;* Yudhistra's *Anantvijay;* Nakul's *Sughosh;* and Sahadev's *Manipushpak.* Lord Vishnu's *shankh* was famous as *Panchjanya.*

There are two kinds of *shankhs* – *vamavart* and *dakshinavart,* according to the direction of the spirals on the conch. In *vamavart,* the spirals wind leftward and the air exit is on the left whereas in *dakshinavart,* the coils wind to right and the air exit is on the right. The shankh with its mouth on the right side, was accepted by Lord Vishnu and those with left openings are dear to Goddess Lakshmi. Thus, both these special forms are considered divine and auspicious. Generally, *dakshinavart shankhs* are rare, so imitations are made. In Rameshwaram, otherwise rare *shankhs* are plentiful here.

The test of the genuine *shankh* lies in holding it close to the ear to hear whether a sonorous drone or its vibration, lingers for a long time. This drone is known as the *anahat nad,* pervades the Universe and is also identified with the mystic syllable *Om,* believed to be inherent in Lord Vishnu's *shankh, Panchjanya,* and in his *chakra* (discus).

During religious ceremonies, after the *Kalash Puja,* the sacred *shankh* is worshipped with flowers and anointed with sandalwood paste, vermilion and topped with *Tulsi* leaves. A flower dipped into *shankh* water, is sprinkled on *puja* items and on oneself. While performing this ritual, a *sloka* is generally recited which ascribes the shankha's base to Chandra; its *kuskhit* or middle to Varuna; its back or *prishtabhag* to Prajapati; and its apex to Ganga-Saraswati. The sloka finally concludes by making obeisance to the *panchjanya shankh* which originated in the ocean and which Lord Vishnu holds in his hands, with the words: 'Thou art omnipresent before all the Gods.'

Strangely, *abhishek* with the *shankh* is performed to all gods except Shiva and Surya. However, while performing *puja,* the *shankh* is one of the important offerings to the deities the final *aarti* is done. Again, it is believed that unless the *shankh* or conch is blown, the temple door should not be opened and anyone who does so becomes deaf.

In natural history, *shankh* or conch is the popular name for many large, shell-bearing sea snails or mollusks. According to *Colliers' Encyclopedia*, the same name is given to large sea-snails – *Busycon carica* and *B.canaliculatum*, which feed on oysters in New England. *Strombus gigas* or Queen Conch (*shankh*), is probably the most important and the largest snail in Florida and the West Indies, measuring a foot in length. Pink pearls are sometimes found within the folds of the queen conch. Amongst *shankhs*, cream or light yellow ones are said to be genuine and those with narrow mouths or openings are recognized to be precious and rare.

From primitive times, *shankhs* and shells have been importantas currency, medicine and food. The *shankh* used in the worship of Goddess Lakshmi, refers to her birth from the ocean and the cowrie shells (*Cypress moneta*), also used in Lakshmi *puja*, to her being the goddess of wealth as these were used as early currency. In Bengal specially, the *shankh* is highly regarded and is blown every evening and on all auspicious occasions as a sign of good omen. Ironically, cowries have been used as dice in games of chance and have caused the downfall of many kingdoms.

In Indian handicrafts, shells are used profusely to make curios and articles like lamp-shades, incense stands, paper-weights, dolls and other decorative items. Beautiful necklaces made from cowries are quite common. In Bengal, bangles made from white shell and known as *shakha*, are worn by married women as an auspicious sign of matrimony.

There are many legends and myths pertaining to the *shankh*. The *Devi Bhagwat* narrates the story of Shankhchud, the demon who was married Tulsi according to *Gandhari* rites. Shankhchud becames so powerful that he held complete sway over even the kingdom of the gods. The gods sought the help of Lord Shiva but Shiva failed to defeat Shankhchud. The reason was the protective amulet which Shankhchud wore, given to him by Lord Krishna which also depended for its power on the chastity of his wife, Tulsi. In order to destroy Shankhchud, Lord Vishnu went to him in the garb of an old man and asked for the amulet as alms. Lord Vishnu then disguised himself as Shankhchud and betrayed Tulsi. Lord Shiva was then able to kill the demon Shankhchud. When Tulsi became aware of the betrayal, she cursed Lord Vishnu and turned him into a black stone. Vishnu retaliated by placing a curse on Tulsi, to turn into a shrub in the jungle . This is the reason why the *shaligram* or ammonite stone found chiefly in the river Gandaki, represents Lord Vishnu and why the *ocimum sanctum*, the *Tulsi* plant, are both worshipped.

It is said that Guatam Buddha was blessed with the symbol of the *shankh* on the soles of his feet. In Roman mythology, the spiraling, one-piece shell of certain sea molluscs, were used as trumpets by the Tritons. In the Ramayana, it says that even Ravana, who abducted Sita, revered the *shankh* and the sentence passed on Hanuman, on being caught in Lanka, was announced by blowing of the *shankh*.

SHRIPHAL ~ COCONUT

Coconut, used so extensively in India in our daily culinary requirements, actually occupies an important place in Indian culture. In all Hindu religious ceremonies, offerings of coconuts along with Betel leaves (*paan*) and Betel nuts (*supari*), is obligatory. It is regarded as symbolic of Ganesh, the god of success and the remover of obstacles.

Before any auspicious function or inauguration or even before using a new car or gadget, a coconut is first broken and the coconut water poured in invocation of success and prosperity. Small pieces of its kernel are then distributed to all present as *prasad* (offering). When a disciple is initiated by a *Guru*, the *Guru* is offered a coconut. Similarly, when a child starts his first lessons, the child offers a coconut to his teacher, requesting him to accept him as his student and bless him in his quest for knowledge. Be it spiritual, academic, the arts or music, the *Guru* or teacher is revered by offerings of coconut on *Guru Purnima* day.

In Hindu marriage ceremonies, the bride carries a coconut

when she is brought to the marriage area by her uncle. Again, on the bride's departure for her husband's house, she takes a coconut in her hand, as a sign of good omen.

The coconut tree is regarded with much veneration because of its multiple utility. Women often take oaths to offer coconuts to the deities if their desire for children is fulfilled. Before a new born is first placed in the decorated cradle during the naming ceremony, a coconut is first decorated and placed in the cradle.

During the *Haldi-Kumkum* ritual of *suhasini* women (whose husbands are alive), coconut, along with Betel leaf and Betel nut is offered to the invitees. Prior to the commencement of a religious ceremonies, the *kalash-staphana* (placing of the pot) is done and a coconut is put on the *kalash* and then it *is* by worshipped to prevent all obstacles. The pinnacles of temples are often made in the shape of a *kalash* and coconut. On *Shravan Poornima* day, coconuts are offered to the sea to appease it. Known as *Narali Poorniama*, this day marks the end of the monsoon.

The coconut is looked upon as a symbol of *brahman*, therefore, while breaking a coconut and using it, at least a tuft should be lretained of the outer coir.

Legend has it that the sage Vishwamitra was the creator of this wonder fruit. When the gods pushed down King Trishanku from heaven, Vishwamitra became angry and as a challenge, decided to create a parallel world. He began to make artificial summer and change the pleasant weather of October into sultry heat which is known as Vishamitra's summer. Moreover, he created coconuts with two eye-like sockets and a beard of coir. Just as he was about to infuse life into the coconuts, Lord Brahma intervened and requested him to stop the project. Vishwamitra agreed but on the condition that the coconut was treated with respect and dignity. He also stipulated that all auspicious ceremonies would be solemnized in its presence. He also stated that if any devout lady ate the seed of a one-eyed coconut, she would be blessed with a child. To make it endure into posterity, he added symbolic power to it.

Coconut is a multi-purpose fruit having medicinal value and is useful in industry too. Due to its glucose content and balance of phosphorus and carbohydrates, it is good for diabetic patients. Coconut water with a few drops of lemon is an easy cure for dehydration. Its sweet water is given to sick people as nourishment and eating the kernel is improves vision. *Vaidyas* (*Ayurvedic* doctors), burn its outer shell to make tooth powder and extract its oil to make ointments for pain alleviation.

Largely featured in cookery, coconut oil is mostly used in south Indian cooking. Coconut oil is used as a cosmetic for luxuriant hair and beautiful skin. A wide assortment of handicrafts are made from its shell and coir. The long fronds are also dried and woven to make fans, mats, curtains and shades, while brooms are made with the thin spikes which are obtained after peeling the leaves.

Sages have compared the coconut to our human body. Initially the kernel remains inseparably attached to the shell, just as humans remain attached to their worldly possessions. But when it dries up, the kernel detaches itself from the shell and we obtain the sweet kernel.

The coconut is revered even by Zoroastrians who use it in their ceremonies. Thus, because of its bounty, the Hindus in particular consider it auspicious fruit and call it *shriphal*.

SUPARI ~ BETEL NUT

Supari or Betel nut, is one item which is indispensable to Hindu rituals. Supari always goes with Betel leaf or *paan*. *Suparis* can be either red or white.

No auspicious ceremony or function is carried out without *supari*. Along with Betel leaf, a coconut and 5 bananas, it is placed on a plate before idols of worship prior to the commencement of religious rites. During the Ganapati festival, before the idol is brought for worship, Betel nut is put on one side to avert any impediment. To offer *supari* and *paan* to anyone, signifies a gesture of honour. Before the commencement of regular ceremonies at a wedding, the bride and the groom offer *paan* with *supari* to the elders, touching their feet and seeking their blessings.

During festivals, when ladies hold functions such as the *Haldi-Kumkum*, especially in south Indian communities, it is the custom to offer *supari* and *paan* to *suhasini* ladies (whose husbands are alive), while giving *Haldi- Kumkum*. Again in the month of *Shravan* when *Tulsi Puja* is performed, every Friday and Sunday, *paan* and *supari* along with other items of worship are placed before the *Tulsi* plant.

After meals it is customary for Indians to distribute grated or flaked supari – this helps digestion and also rounds up the meal with its nutty taste. Many varieties of supariare available; for example, sweet, scented, plain or mixed with other savoury spices catering to the gourmets.

The word *supari* is, unfortunately, used by the underworld as well. In their code language, 'to give supari' to someone signifies hiring an assassin to commit a crime against theat person, thus abusing the rich, cultural and sacred connotations of the Betel nut.

Supari has been popular and been a significant part of our religious, social and cultural lives since ancient times. In Maharashta it is also called *Poogiphal*. It is surmised that the word *supari* originated in the Kanarese language.

In Maharashtra, *supari* plantations are abundant in the districts of Karwar, Ratnagiri, Thana as well as Goa. The Betel nut of the Karwar district is quite famous. Betel nut plantations are also found in Bengal, Kerala, Mysore and Tamil Nadu. Outside India, plantations exist in China, Malaysia Sri Lanka and Mayanmar.

A hot and damp climate is required to grow *supari*. It grows normally on the seashore and does not survive if planted away from it. *Supari* trees planted at the foot of hills are generally valleys with water and where the fruit is protected from strong winds. There are different techniques in use to cultivate the supari tree.

The Betel nut is plucked before it is ripe. Then the outer fibre is removed and the nut boiled in water till it is ready to be extracted. The nuts are then dried in the sun and shielded from overnight dew. The processing of Betel nuts is an indigenous craft calling for mastery and skill.

Kath or *Catechu*, is made from the distilled essence that remains after boiling the Betel nuts. It is the ingredient in a prepared and stuffed *paan* which imparts the bitter tang and coats the mouth red. Singers use *paan* as it is said to improve their voices. *Supari* is exported in large quantities and is a great revenue earner.

SWASTIKA ~ SACRED SYMBOL

Prince Harry's party outfit, a Nazi uniform with an armband featuring the *swastika*, created great commotion, some leaders even demanding an all-Europe ban on the symbol because it was used on the flag as the Nazi emblem during Hitler's regime.

But in Hinduism, the *swastika* is highly revered and holds great religious significance, second only to *Om*. Unlike *Om*, the *swastika* is not a syllable or a letter. It is an ancient mystic, auspicious symbol. The word *swastika* is believed to be an amalgam of the Sanskrit words *su* (well) *asti* (it is) *ka* (grammatical non ending) – i.e. 'It is well'. As per Sanskrit grammar, the words *su* and *asati* when combined, become *swasti* just as *su* and *aastam* become *swagatam*, meaning 'welcome'. So the literal meaning of swastika means 'let good prevail'. The word *svasti* is used before and after pronouncing the sacred syllable *Om* and during sacrificial ceremonies.

In Hindu lore, the *swastika* as an auspicious symbol, is believed to have originated from the two fire sticks of the *vedic* sacrificial fire, which were always placed in the form of a cross. Perhaps it may have also been derived from the wheel symbolically reduced to four spokes and set at right angles to indicate the cardinal points, with the right end of the horizontal bar bent downwards at right angles, those of the other three arms also bent in the same way and following the same clock-wise direction.

The right hand 'male' *swastika,* representing the vernal sun, is considered auspicious. Whereas, the left hand 'female' *swastika* (following the anti-clockwise direction), representing the autumnal sun, is considered inauspicious. As a fire and sun symbol, it is also called the Fire Cross or the Solar Cross. The equal armed cross did not have any particular significance in Hinduism but the *swastika* became important.

The auspicious *swastika,* is also a symbol of good luck and is often found marked on objects. Even in the epic *Ramayana,* there is mention of utensils for domestic use being marked with this symbol. Apart from using this symbol in all religious ceremonies, it is used as a motif in textiles, floor decorations and *mehendi* designs on the hands and feet of women. In Maharashtra, during the monsoon, women honour the *swastika* symbol by drawing it on floors and worshipping it.

In *yoga,* the *svastikasana* (posture) is practiced while meditating, when two crosses are formed – one by squatting with the legs crossed (one on the other), and the other with arms crossed over the breast. The *swastika* has been an important symbol for *tantriks* too.

The *swastika* is said to be marked on the hood of the Cobra, and is, in fact, often found associated with the culture of snake-worshipping people like the Nagas and is thus looked upon with reverence.

The symbol of the *swastika* has been discovered in countries as far apart as Egypt, Greece, China and Japan. The European *Fylfot* of mediaeval times was in fact the same symbol. The *swastika* is sometimes found engraved on church bells in Europe and in England. *Fylfot* of the Buddhists, found on Buddhist images, is regarded as an emblem of Lord Buddha's heart.

Probably the *swastika* was a common symbol and was used as a magical sign by the Aryans before their diaspora to India and Europe. Besides being a spiritual symbol, the *swastika* was also played an important part in the lives of the people. Some scholars say that in ancient times, forts were built in the shape of a grid or a maze resembling the *swastika*, for defensive purposes. The idea was to make it difficult for the enemy to storm into all parts of the fort simultaneously. Needless to say, this intriguing form was used as a blueprint for building forts called *suvatsu*.

In a conventional fort, the fall of one of the gates, led to the capture and massacre of the inhabitants. But, with the *swastika* grid, the fall of any one of the four gates could still keep the other three-fourths of the fort safe. The *swastika* as a blueprint for fort construction, can perhaps be explained from an etymological point. In Sanskrit, *vasa* means 'to inhabit' and 'vastu' means habitation, while 'su' means good – hence the amalgam to create *swastu*, meaning 'a good habitation'. The term *swasta* means 'calm' or 'peaceful'. Thus the term *swastika* might have been derived from the nomenclature for a defensive structure which ultimately led to mean good habitation.

This strategic defensive arrangement in the shape of a *swastika* or maze, is corroborated by the military practice of *Chakra-vyuha*, which was used during the *Mahabharata* war, an episode in which Arjuna's son Abhimanyu was killed. In the *Chakra-Vyuha*, the army was arranged in a circular grid which the enemy had to break into. The *Chakra-Vyuha* was an effective trap as once the enemy entered it, it was difficult to escape unless he knew the secret of the exit, as was the case with Abhimanyu in the *Mahabharata*.

When Subhadra, was pregnant with Abhimanyu, Sri Krishna, her brother, would take her out for rides in his chariot. To entertain his sister, Krishna related many of his adventures. Once, Krishna began narrating his experience of the *Chakra-vyuha* technique and how one by one the various circles could be penetrated. Subhadra, finding the topic uninteresting, dozed off. But Abhimanyu, inside his mother's womb, listened eagerly. But as destined, seeing Subhadra napping, Sri Krishna stopped at the seventh step of the *Chakra-Vyuha* and gave up his narration.

Abhimanyu grew up to be a brave warrior and remembered whatever Krishna had narrated while he was still in his mother's womb. During the *Mahabharata* war, Abhimanyu volunteered to break the *Chakra-Vyuha* set up by the Kauravas. Despite his incomplete knowledge of the technique, he entered the grid and overcame all the circles of the army till he came to the seventh one. Alas! He had no knowledge of breaking out beyond this point. He fought valiantly but was no match against the maze of the Kauravas and so met his end in battle.

TAEL or GHEE ~ ANOINTING OIL

Tael or oil, is important in our rituals and in Indian culture through many usages. Oil, in the form of cosmetics and medicines, is found in great variety, even in ancient India. However, animal fats are forbidden in rituals.

For *pujas*, oil is indispensable because without it no *diya* or lamp can be lit. Scented and coloured preparations of oil or *ghee* (clarified butter), are popular. Oil is applied to the head and body of a person before and also after a bath to invigorate the body. Ancient literature states that diseases do not approach those who do physical exercise and anoint their limbs with oil. Infants are also massaged with mustard or coconut oil, depending on the regional use.

Oil plays an essential part in all Hindu purificatory rites or *sanskaras*. For example, at the hair-parting ceremony called *Simantonnayana*, the husband parts the hair of his wife beginning from the front upwards. But, before this, oblations are made into the fire and the wife, having performed her ablutions, fragrant oil is poured onto her head. Then the husband parts her hair reciting the sacred *mantras* appropriate for this ceremony.

Immediately after birth, infants are rubbed with oil and then washed. In the ceremony called *Medha Janana*, honey and *ghee* are mixed together and the father gently touches the mouth of the child with a golden spoon dipped in this mixture. Again, at the time of *Chudakarana* or *Chaula*, the ceremony of first tonsure or cutting of hair, the child is anointed with oil and washed. During *Upanayana*, when a boy is invested with the sacred thread, he is anointed with oil and *haridra*.

In the *Haridralepana* ceremony prior to the marriage rites, the bride and the groom are smeared with a mixture of turmeric and oil. This signifies purification and auspiciousness.

In some communities, one of the preliminary wedding ceremonies is to have the bride rotate the grinding stone *chakra* holding its wooden handle with the help of 5 *suhasini* (whose husbands are alive) women. All of them take small quantities of *udad dal* (black gram) and mixed with oil, insert it into the small hole of the grinding stone to make flour. During *Upanayana* and also at the wedding ceremony, the stone which the *batu* or novitiate and the bridal couple have to touch, is first anointed with oil. Again, the bride's brother smears the hands of the bride with *ghee* and sprinkles puffed rice upon her.

Unction or anointing with oil, is a minor ritual, which possesses considerable significance in the history of sacramental religion. In early cultures, animal and vegetable fats and oils were used. The principle of anointment according to primitive psychology, was connected to the investment of a divine force in sacred persons, objects and places and later, the gods, their temples, representatives and apparatus. In its sacred applications, anointing oil was the vehicle of a sacred or Divine life or vital essence. The sacramental principle is thus the controlling factor in the theory of anointing. The methods of transmitting the sacred essence to the unguent are material contact, magical and religious formulas, intention, blessing and prayer.

Thus, amongst the Hindus, during *Antyeshti*, that is rites performed upon death, the body is washed and anointed with sandal-paste, oil and turmeric. The forehead of a dying man, if possible, is smeared with sacred mud from the Ganges. At the burial of the urn or throwing the ashes into a holy river, the chief mourner anoints himself with *ghee*. The anointing of the dead is based on the principle that the dead 'may depart clean and in neat attire from this world of cares'.

As in *Vedic* times, priests and worshippers, wash and then anoints themselves with oil or *ghee* before performing religious rites. The institutor of a ceremony also anoints himself. During festivals like *Sankranti* and *Diwali*, it is the custom for everyone to take a bath at dawn and to apply oil on the body before bathing.

Among the Hindus, on particular days allotted for different gods or goddesses, such as Saturdays for Maruti, the monkey-god or Lord Shani (Saturn), people religiously offer oil in the respective temples.

The images in temples are bathed, anointed and dressed by the priests daily. For this purpose, *vilepana* is one of the essential offerings presented by worshippers. Also, sacred stones like the *salagrama*, are also anointed and decorated by *Vaishnavites* and the *linga* worshippers of Shiva.

In the *nirudha-pasubanadha* rite, the tree from which the sacrificial post was to be cut, was first anointed and the victim, after being rubbed with oil and turmeric, and washed, was anointed with *ghee*. In the *yagna* sacrifice, the ram is rubbed with oil, bathed, covered with *akshata* and garlanded. At the *Durga puja* festival, a banana tree is bathed and anointed with several kinds of scented oils.

In Buddhism too, at the ordination of a Buddhist priest, his hair is touched with oil before being cut. The important ceremony of *abhisheka*, the royal coronation or consecration, is also in principle, a form of unction. Holy water which has 18 ingredients with which the consecration is done, includes *ghee* or oil as an important item. The anointing of kings and priests combine several principles such as the transmission of sanctity, power, and new life as also protection in the performance of his office.

It is interesting that the consecration of building by means unction is a well-developed feature of Hindu ritual. There is a ceremony like the laying of a foundation stone, in which a piece of wood or *sanku*, is decorated and anointed – being thereby animated with the spirit of the god Vastupurusha, who then becomes the tutelary deity of the house.

Moreover, when the main entrance is put up, the wood work is anointed with sandalwood oil and worshipped. The same ceremony is performed over the ridge–plate and the well, and for the house generally, when it is first entered into.

Oil has extensively culinary and medical uses. Sandalwood oil is popular on account of its fragrance. Ayurvedic medicinal oils too are popular and effective for body pains. Magical unguents, to which potency was imparted through *mantras*, were and stll are, used to inspire love and to prevent or cure disease. The *amrta* oil made men strong and women lovely; it ensured offspring, averted misfortune, promoted prosperity and guaranteed long life. Its manufacture was preceded by purificatory rites. The *priest*, before anointing himself, was supposed to think of the *Chiranjivans* or 'the long-lived', the seven half-divine persons.

Cosmetics have used oils from ancient times. The application of unguents to the skin and hair have become regular practices today. Vegetable oils, with balsams, vegetable pastes and powders, like turmeric, sandal and mustard, sawdust and flour, or the sap and pollen of plants, were all used. Perfumes were usually prepared in the form of ointments.

The action of oil is to produce a sensation of comfort and well-being while making the joints and muscles supple. Oil closes the pores of the skin and partially represses perspiration. Its cosmetic use soon acquired aesthetic associations. The use of unguents as the vehicle of perfumes, became a luxury among the Persians, Hindus, Greeks, and Romans. Among early people however, it was common practice to use oils for personal enhancement, on both ordinary and ceremonial occasions.

The principle of communion with the deity by means of anointing the sacred symbol or the worshipper himself, is more apparent in the elementary stages of worship. The anointing oil transmits the sacredness latent within it in two directions – towards the worshipper and towards god.

TULSI ~ HOLY BASIL

Tulsi or *Ocimum sanctum*, is a revered plant in India. It is an erect herb about 75cms high, with branches. The leaves grow on opposite sides of the stem and are highly aromatic. It has small purple or red flower clusters and its seeds too are yellow or red. There are two varieties of *Tulsi*, one known as *Ram Tulsi*, which is white and the other is *Krishna Tulsi*, which is black.

Hindus believe the *Tulsi* to be pervaded by the divinity of Vishnu and his consort, Lakshmi, hence it is venerated by every Hindu, specially the Vaishnavites. It is venerated so deeply that it is normally planted in the courtyard of Hindu homes and worshipped. It is believed that it wards off evil spirits which do not dare to come to the place where *Tulsi* grows. Also called *Haripriya*, a Sanskrit term meaning 'dear to Lord Vishnu' and *Bhutaghni* or the killer of demons.

Legend says that Tulsi, in her former life, was Vrinda, the daughter of a giant named Nemi or Kalanemi. She was married to the demon Jalandar, who acquired this name because he was born of the sweat which Shiva had thrown from his brow into the ocean when he perspired at being insulted by Indra. Born in water or *jala*, Jalandar claimed as his birthright, suzerainty of the ocean and demanded back from Indra the 14 treasures which were churned out of the ocean (during the second incarnation of Vishnu). But the king of gods, Indra, refused. Jalandhar then worshipped Brahma by performing severe penance and Brahma, pleased with him, granted him the boon of freedom from death as long as his wife remained faithful.

Jalandhar took advantage of this boon and looted and plundered Amaravati, the capital of *Swarga* or Heaven. The gods, now in trouble, sought the help of Vishnu, who disguised as Jalandhar, succeeded in seducing Vrinda. The moment this came to pass, Jalandhar's head was severed by Indra and it fell next to Vrinda. The chaste Vrinda was a great devotee of Lord Vishnu. Shocked at this deception by the god she adored and respected, Vrinda cursed Vishnu for his deceit. She pronounced that Vishnu would turn into a black stone. Vishnu retaliated and cursed Vrinda saying that she would become the shrub *Tulsi* in the jungle.

This is the reason why Vishnu, in the form of *shaligrama*, the ammonite stone, is found chiefly in the river Gandaki and Vrinda as the Tulsi plant. But their innate love for each other is so sacred and pure that a mock marriage is performed between the idol of Lord Krishna and the Tulsi , by placing a *shaligrama* near the plant every year in the auspicious month of *Kartik*.

Whoever perfumes this mock marriage ceremony, taking Tulsi as his daughter, gets all the credit of performing a *kanyadaan*. This ceremony marks the commencement of the annual marriage season for orthodox Hindus.

The value of *Tulsi* is so great that when Lord Krishna was weighed, all the jewels possessed by Satyabhama could not outweigh him. But, when Rukmini placed a single *Tulsi* leaf on the scale, lo! up went the scale owith Lord Krishna.

Tulsi is so adorable to god that for offerings of food or *naivedya,* the *Tulsi* leaf is indispensable. It is waved 5 times before the *naivedya* and the gods, then small pieces of the leaf are put in each of the preparations denoting that god has accepted the *naivedya* and the family can partake of it. Tulsi leaves are used to make *panchamrita* (nectar of 5) which is a mixture of milk, curd, ghee, honey and sugar.

It is taboo to throw away the dried Tulsi plant, other than in a river or a pond. During eclipses, Hindus put *Tulsi* leaves into food and water to save them from pollution. This age-old belief still persists among women in India. *Tulsi* leaves and water from the Ganges, are put into the mouth of a dying Hindu to earn salvation. Furthermore, the Tulsi is not only sacred for *pujas* but is also indispensable for ancestor worship, when oblations known as *tarpan,* to deceased forefathers, require Sesamum and Basil.

Tulsi leaves are said to have great medicinal value and are used to cure cough, cold, fever and respiratory complaints. *Tulsi* seeds (two spoonfuls), soaked in water overnight and taken in the morning, is a good remedy for cough. Again, if a patient drinks a cup of water boiled with *Tulsi* leaves, it can help cure Malaria. To make water germ-free, people put *Tulsi* leaves into water jugs. Many people eat *Tulsi* leaves first thing in the morning to maintain good health. Because of its aromatic smell, it also keeps reptiles and insects away. Thus the *Tulsi* has many attributes.

The Tulsi plant is so sacred to the Hindus that a lamp or *diya* is lit near it daily and this prayer spoken: 'I adore the *Tulsi,* in whose roots are all the places of pilgrimage, in whose center are all the deities, and in whose upper branches are all the *Vedas.*'

VIBHUTI ~ SACRED ASH

One of the sacred substances associated with our religious life is *vibhuti* or ash. This probably originated from the sacrificial fires used during religious ceremonies. The ash being the remnant of the fire or Agni of the *homa* or *yagna*, it is considered to be sacred and to have great power. Agni has been revered and worshipped as a god from the Vedic ages. More than the Sun, Agni or Fire was more useful and nearer, so men held it in high esteem.

Sacrifices were performed to appease the gods and for some gain. They were performed by priests who made oblations of clarified butter, coconut, etc. into the sacrificial fires. It was assumed that these offerings into the *homa*, were carried through the flames to the gods. Agni or fire, acted as a mediator between man and the gods. Fire was to the Hindu, a visible embodiment not only of heat but of all the other forces of nature. Thus, the ash from its embers was considered sacred.

In ancient times, *homa* was performed daily, even at home. Even today we perform the *Gana Homa* before an auspicious

WORSHIP Essentials For Puja

inauguration or on the eve of Ganapati *puja*, before installing the idol. The ashes from the *Gana Homa* is generally known as *raksha*. This black soot or ash is applied to the foreheads to protect one from harm.

An orthodox Hindu usually marks his forehead with the sacred signs (called *pundra* or *tilak*) of his own particular sect. The mark is sometimes perpendicular and sometimes circular or three horizontal lines (*trpundra*). After bathing, a Shiva worshipper marks his forehead with three horizontal lines of ash or *bhasma* taken from the domestic hearth. He also rubs it on other parts of his body while praying to Shiva. A Vaishanavite, on the other hand, has vertical markings on his forehead, which denote the impress of the god Vishnu's feet. It consists of two upright lines joined by a curve at the bottom. Generally it is made using earth brought form Dwarka or with Sandalwood paste (*Gopichandan*).

Vibhuti is used as a charm too, by sages having spiritual powers. Some are said to have performed miracles by giving their devotees a pinch of *vibhuti* or ash to save them from difficulties, diseases or even their lives. We get evidence of this from the life of Shri Sai Baba of Shirdi. Even today, at Shirdi, we find the *dhuni* or sacrificial fireplace where a perpetual fire was kept burning by Sai Baba. From the embers of the eternal *dhuni*, sacred ash (usually called *udi*), is distributed to devotees. Shri Satya Saibaba of Phutapathi is also well known for performing miracles with *vibhuti*.

Again, in the Himalayas, one of the most portent charms against evil spirits is known as the 'ashes formula' (*vibhuti mantra*). Ash is smeared on the patient thrice and then rubbed off so as to disperse the dangerous influence. In south India, patients of the Saiva sect are also rubbed with sacred ash while a charm is recited. Then again, a bath of ash or *vibhuti* is one of the modes of purification used by the Lingayats.

In the *Puranas*, we find instances of ascetics having turned men to ash with their spiritual powers. The *Holi* festival also commemorates the occasion when Lord Shiva, engaged in meditation, scorched Kama-dev, the god of love, to ash through a flash of rage from his middle eye. Also, Sage Kapila burnt to ashes the 60,000 sons of King Sagar. From the bonfire lit during *Holi*, ash is taken home and treated as sacred.

On Ash Wednesday in the Roman Catholic Church, every member of the congregation comes forward to the altar to be marked with the sign of the cross, made with ash from the palm leaves used on Palm Sunday.

In modern times when domestic hearths are a rarity, religious minded people procure this sacred *vibhuti* or ash from temples or their *Gurus* and with great faith, apply it on their foreheads every day.

ACKNOWLEDGEMENTS

Once again, I owe my late husband, S.B. Sashital, special thanks. He always stood by me and spared no effort in helping me to bring out this book.

My heartfelt thanks to Mr. M.V. Kamath, for giving his valuable time to write the Foreword to my book. I reiterate that I have always regarded him as my Guru and shall forever remain indebted to him for his generosity.

We find the glory of worship or *puja* aptly expressed by Lord Krishna in the *Bhagvad Gita* where he says:

patram pushpam phalam toyam yo me bhaktya prayachchhati,
tad-aham bhakty-upahritam asnami prayatatmanahi
[If anyone offers me with devotion a leaf, a flower, a fruit, and water, I receive that, offered in devotion by the persons whose soul is disciplined.]

I hope that these pages will serve to renew knowledge of our *puja* traditions and add meaning to your personal rituals of worship.

120

ABOUT THE AUTHOR

Born in the little town of Udupi in South Kanara, **Meera Sashital** has been a freelance writer for over 50 years. Based in Mumbai, she has written for a broad spectrum of newspapers and magazines in India. A Philosophy graduate from Calcutta University, circumstances compelled her to give up her dream of further education for a time. But, always ready to face life's challenges in a positive spirit, she did go on to complete her Masters in Sociology, ten years later. She also gained her *Sangit Visharad* from the Bengal Music College, Calcutta, and utilizing her knack for languages, she learnt both French and German.

Through the years, her love of writing has remained her abiding passion. Meera has authored four books prior to this one – *Gems from Mythology; Rosary of Saints; Strewn Pearls* and *Moral Legends from the Epics and Puranas*.

Meera Sashital can be reached at: meersashy27@yahoo.com

Made in the USA
San Bernardino, CA
09 February 2016